What No One Ever Tells You About

INVESTING IN REAL ESTATE

D0976286

Robert J. Hill II, Esq.

Dearborn™
Trade Publishing
A **Kaplan Professional** Company

This publication is designed to provide accurate and authoritative information in regard to the subject matter covered. It is sold with the understanding that the publisher is not engaged in rendering legal, accounting, or other professional service. If legal advice or other expert assistance is required, the services of a competent professional should be sought.

Vice President and Publisher: Cynthia A. Zigmund
Acquisitions Editor: Mary B. Good
Senior Project Editor: Trey Thoelcke
Interior Design: Lucy Jenkins
Cover Design: Scott Rattray, Rattray Design
Typesetting: the dotted i

Published by Dearborn Trade Publishing
A Kaplan Professional Company

Printed in the United States of America

05 06 07   10 9 8 7 6 5 4 3 2 1

Library of Congress Cataloging-in-Publication Data

Hill, Robert J., 1973–
    What no one ever tells you about investing in real estate : real-life advice from 101 successful investors / Robert J. Hill, II.
      p.   cm.
    Includes bibliographical references and index.
    ISBN 0-7931-9516-0
    1. Real estate investment.   2. Real estate management.   3. Landlord and tenant. I. Title.
    HD1382.5.H548 2005
    332.63′24—dc22

                                                   2004015646

In memory of my grandfather, Burkhardt John Zoeller, Sr., a welder and real estate investor who preached the value of education, and in honor of the children of real estate investors everywhere—you are wise beyond your years.

CONTENTS

PART 2   FINDING GOOD INVESTMENT DEALS   57

Finally! Here's a book about the "real" side of owning and renting property, with no sugar coating. *What No One Ever Tells You about Investing in Real Estate* by Rob Hill is a must-read for anyone who owns rental property today or considers buying it for the future. With pathos and humor, this book lets you know about the "real deal" of managing tenants; its 112 stories open your eyes in a highly entertaining way.

Do you enjoy the popular reality shows on TV today? I've always said that owning rental property is much more intriguing than any of these shows. Turn to these easy-to-read tales of tenant and contractor adventures because they have it all—drama, humor, love, excitement, tragedy, and even violence. From lying, cheating repair people to swat teams destroying a home to delusional tenants to evictions laced with emotional roller-coaster rides and the best in landlord lore—you're about to experience it all.

Rob Hill and his family have been immersed in real estate for decades and are excellent managers. Like the Hill family, many of the property owners whose stories you're about to read are friends of mine. They'd agree with me that Rob has done an excellent job of collecting a variety of true management occurrences—some funny, some real nightmares. Yet the stories all have a highly practical side; they offer real-life lessons about *what to do* and *what not to do* when managing rental properties.

I encourage you to cherish this as a great opportunity for you—the soon-to-be-intrigued reader of *What No One Ever Tells You about Investing in Real Estate*—to learn the inside scoop about landlord-ing. Buy and manage rental properties yourself so you, too, can enjoy the "real" ride in the trenches—and have your own great tales to tell, landlords and landladies.

Robert Shemin, author of:
Secrets of a Millionaire Investor
Secrets of a Millionaire Landlord
Unlimited Riches: Making Your Fortune in Real Estate Investing
Secrets of Buying and Selling Real Estate

PREFACE

Experience keeps a dear school, yet fools will learn in no other.
Benjamin Franklin in *Poor Richard's Almanac*

This book is full of mistakes, full of successes, and full of experience. On the following pages, successful real estate investors from across America share their stories with you. Their stories are completely true, although when requested, I have given some contributors pseudonyms "to protect the innocent."

You'll find on these pages the good, bad, happy, and sad experiences of ordinary investors. If you invest in real estate, learn from them. If you don't invest in real estate, laugh with them.

As the children of active real estate investors, my brother Mark and I have become wise beyond our years in this area. Our parents have been active real estate investors for almost 20 years, so Mark and I, too, have been active investors for almost 20 years.

Note: Active real estate investors give blood, sweat, and tears to add "sweat equity" to their properties. If it's humanly possible and anywhere close to being legal, then odds are that an active real estate investor will do it.

As teenagers, Mark and I didn't collect rent, pay taxes, or find properties, but, heck, we didn't have cars. Still, before we could legally drive, we helped our parents hammer, level, saw, plumb, mow, and generally rehab more than a few properties. We weren't always happy about doing it but—unlike many children of our generation—we spent a lot of time with our parents and we learned many valuable skills.

Today, we both make our living in the real estate realm. Mark is a Realtor and I am a real estate attorney. Every day, we deal with the "paper" aspects of real estate investing, but we know much more from real life experience. Thanks Mom and Dad!

My grandfather, Burkhardt (Pop) John Zoeller, Sr., was apparently the first real estate investor in our family. Because his father died and his mother needed help supporting her four children, Pop dropped out of school and started working full-time when he was 13. After he attended welding school and built patrol torpedo boats during World War II, Pop bought his first investment property—a vacant lot on Main Street in Louisville, Kentucky. He built a cinderblock structure on it and started his own welding business.

Over the years, his welding income supported his wife, Opal, and their five children, plus it allowed him to buy many more pieces of property. He invested in apartment buildings, houses, and vacant land lots. At 84, he reluctantly retired from his welding shop and lived on income from the many properties that he owned and still managed.

Because he believed that he could have gotten farther with an education, Pop always urged his family, friends, and anyone else who would listen to get one. Ironically, like many of the investors featured in this book, he did quite well without formal schooling. Perhaps a lack of formal education, official degrees, and letters behind their names has allowed such people to see things more clearly. In the words of Sir Winston Churchill: "They all said it couldn't be done; then along came a man who didn't know, and he did it."

On a practical, applied level, real estate investors can certainly learn from each other, and, perhaps quietly, laugh at each other's mistakes. Members of the Real Estate Investors of Nashville (REIN) really learn from and laugh at each other's mistakes during their annual Christmas party. Each December, they gather to share punch and cookies and listen to "horror" stories about real estate investment experiences where worst-case scenarios became realities. Usually, the president of REIN contacts a few investors in advance and invites them to lead the storytelling, but anyone who attends can stand up and share stories.

And what stories they share! Stories about stolen decks and intimately rocked commodes make us laugh out loud. Like modern Aesops, the storytellers also share the lessons that they learned from each experience. As a result, every person there—even those who just listen—can recall their own horror stories. They can take comfort in knowing that they're not alone when it comes to making mistakes. Indeed, they can begin to wonder if they are, perhaps, much better off than they first thought. Thanks to this Christmas party, the members of REIN laugh about and put many "horrors" behind them. It's their way of starting each new year relieved, inspired, and ready for new possibilities.

Last December, as I listened and laughed with my fellow REIN members, I decided that I wanted to write a book about their experiences—and the experiences of similar investors. When I got home that night, I surfed the Internet to see if anyone else had already written a book like this one, and my research indicated that no one had. Just then, as I thought about it, I remembered reading a similar book in 1995. I had purchased a copy of Rosemary Fuller Thornton's book, *The Reality of Real Estate: What You Don't Know about Investing in Real Estate Can Bankrupt You,* as a gift for my parents. In it, Rosemary used her razor wit to describe her family's torturous experiences on a dead-end adventure down the road of real estate riches. It is a work of satire, one real estate investor's black comedy masterpiece. My parents, already experienced investors, recognized many truths in it and laughed wholeheartedly. These two poems that Rosemary wrote really capture the essence of her experience.

> *My apartment sucked my wallet dry,*
> *And still my losses multiply.*
> *I worked so hard with diligence—*
> *And this year's profits aren't four cents.*

And:

> *I think that I shall never see,*
> *A tenant act responsibly.*
> *There are a few, especially kind,*
> *The rest, they make me lose my mind.*
> *I work so hard to clean and scrub—*
> *And then I rent to Beelzebub.*

If you feel like Rosemary did, don't give up. Instead, read *this* book. Intended to inspire your real estate investing, *What No One Ever Tells You about Investing in Real Estate* shouldn't scare you away. Rather, it should give you a flavor of what really happens through its 112 real-life stories.

The stories in this book come from active real estate investors. People just like you. People who have seen, survived, and even succeeded in good, bad, happy, and sad situations. I hope that their experiences can help you do the right thing.

Read about the good situations and know that you can achieve great things. Read about the bad situations and know that you have not suffered alone. Read about the happy situations and smile. Read about the sad situations and see how you can make things better for yourself.

If you want to invest in real estate—or if you already invest in real estate—this is your opportunity to learn from other real estate investors. If laughter is truly the best medicine, then be sure to laugh aloud at their stories. As you laugh at their stories, think about your own experiences. Maybe you have stories to share with other investors. (See the Author's Note for details on becoming a future contributor.)

ACKNOWLEDGMENTS

First, I have to thank all of the successful real estate investors who made mistakes, learned their lessons, and shared their stories with me.

Second, I have to thank my editorial team.

- Mary B. Good, who believed in this book even as deadlines changed and passed
- Barbara McNichol, who quickly and professionally crafted this book
- Sherry Sterling, who carefully collected permissions and proofread everything
- Amber L. Ferguson, who patiently helped with day-to-day book activities

Finally, I would like to thank fellow attorney, author, and investor, Robert Shemin, who long ago invited me to experience his investor "boot camp" and later introduced me to Mary B. Good at Dearborn Trade Publications.

Without the wonderful work of these fine people, there would be no book.

ATTENTION REAL ESTATE INVESTORS!

You have made mistakes, you have learned lessons, and you have succeeded.

If you've realized something new, you have a story. Good. Bad. Happy. Sad. Please tell me your stories so I can share them with other investors.

Need something to jog your memory? Think about these questions.

- What has been your best real estate deal?
- What has been your worst real estate deal?
- What has been your biggest surprise as an investor?
- If you started over today, what would you do differently?
- If you started over today, what would you like to hear from me?

Send your stories via

E-Mail: Stories@HarpringHill.com
Toll-Free Fax: 877-636-6361
Internet: http://www.realestatestories.com

I look forward to reading your stories. Meanwhile, happy investing!

PART 1

LANDLORD WOES
AND VICTORIES

■ ■ ■

When you hear the phrase *real estate investing,* what comes to mind first?

If you're not an investor, then when you think of landlords and tenants, you probably grimace. Landlords are the subject of many jokes and parodies. It seems we hear almost as many landlord jokes as lawyer jokes and doctor jokes these days. In the popular media, landlords are often portrayed as hapless bumblers or miscreants who neglect or abuse their tenants. Why are landlords portrayed so badly?

After all, landlords have tremendous power. They take care of their tenants' homes and, in a pseudoparental manner, they sometimes take care of tenants themselves. Landlords keep their tenants' homes looking pretty outside and working properly inside. When something doesn't look right or doesn't work right, tenants turn to their landlords. Yet, when the first of the month arrives, tenants clutch their checkbooks and brace their checking accounts. The landlord cometh! As with their lawyers and dentists, tenants usually interact with their landlords only when they're suffering or losing something precious—like their money.

When you buy your first great rental property, you may look forward to being a landlord and learning what real estate investing is really about. You start managing your great piece of real estate, and you also start wondering why you ever thought this experience would be great. The grass grows high, and the credit scores fall low. When your tenants truly have issues, you're not sure if you can maintain your sanity, much less your great property.

Relax—you're not alone. Most successful real estate investors have been landlords at some time or other, and many continue to be landlords. They have dealt with day-to-day property management issues, so they understand that real estate investing operates as a business.

Therefore, if you want to be a successful real estate investor, you should know about the *business* of property management. You must know and comply with a seemingly endless number of local, state, and federal ordinances, rules, regulations, codes, and laws. You must set and collect rents, deposits, fines, and fees in a timely manner. You must deal with immediate emergencies. You must attract, screen, humor, cajole, and sometimes evict tenants. You must repair or replace buildings and other items on your property or find qualified professionals who can do this work for you. You have to do everything possible to prevent injuries. And you'd better have adequate property, liability, management, and disaster insurance coverage, because chances are you'll need it someday.

Landlords often have the most interesting stories to tell. They deal with "average Joe" tenants every day. Quite often, they've been there, done that, and taken home the T-shirt. But that's not to say that they're never surprised. Several of the stories in this section deal with surprises—like disappearing tenants or tenants with illicit lifestyles. Other stories reveal how creative landlords prevent tenant trickery and increase their profits.

If you're a landlord, read, learn, and laugh. If you're a tenant, read and laugh—but don't get any crazy ideas!

1. LANDLORD, BEWARE

Your best deals could be the ones you *don't* do.

■ ■ ■

When investor Joyce Bone bought a quadraplex in Atlanta, she believed that it showed a lot of financial promise. In retrospect, it proved to have a promise going for it but not much else.

After she purchased the property, unit A had been abandoned, and unit B had also become vacant. Joyce soon discovered that the tenant in unit C had *no* intention of paying rent but *every* intention of hating the world—his twin brother had recently been executed for murder in Texas. She asked him to leave, which he did. That left one tenant in unit D.

Because the quadraplex was nearly vacant, Joyce decided to go ahead and rehab it completely. So she told the tenant in unit D that she wouldn't renew his lease. When she told him the news, he turned around and sued her. Why? Because he had established a used car business and was running it out of his unit—and out of the building's parking lot. Clearly, he had a viable business interest in keeping his lease no matter what his landlord wanted. He took special measures to protect it, to the point of behaving badly. For example, one time after Joyce and an appraiser visited the property, he claimed that she was stalking him and had her served with a protective order.

Joyce eventually took the disagreement with the tenant in unit D to court. She won an $8,500 judgment against him but, as she says, "Court is a scary place for an innocent person."

After her cleanup efforts, Joyce was able to sell the quadraplex within six months for a $25,000 profit. Despite making a profit, Joyce declares that "buying this quad was definitely not worth it—a deal better left undone."

2. CASUAL CHAT LEADS TO NEW TENANT

Be a good listener—you never know where your next tenant will come from.

■ ■ ■

As Calvin Keeton played pool against a stranger in Nashville, he was concentrating on his shots and only half-listening to his opponent's words. Then Calvin heard him say, "So you fix houses and then rent them?"

"Yes, I do," he replied.

Calvin then heard him say, "Well, I may be interested in a house for my girlfriend."

At that moment, Calvin thought little of this remark. So many questions from strangers like the pool player led to nothing. So he was surprised when he received a phone call two days later. The voice of his pool-playing opponent was asking, "Can I look at the house you're working on? It would be for my girlfriend."

Calvin was impressed to get the call from this man, but he didn't get too excited, knowing that often people express interest that never pans out. But he wanted to oblige, so he went ahead and gave the caller directions to his rental home.

Two days after that, while playing another game of pool, Calvin's opponent offered, "I like the house and want to rent it."

"Well," Calvin thought, "he's talking the talk, but will he walk the walk?" Then he saw cash hit the pool table.

"Here's her first month's rent, her last month's rent, and $500 to let her in. I'll pay each month's rent to you ahead of the due date. I also want to buy some freestanding closets for her extra clothes. I'll let you know in advance when she decides to move. You can keep the money that I've paid you and keep the closets, too."

This time, he had Calvin's complete attention.

Shortly after, the girlfriend moved in and stayed only three months, but at the end of that time, Calvin had the rent money in his hands, the freestanding closets in his rental house, and a smile of satisfaction on his face.

3. FREE RENT PAYS OFF IN UNUSUAL WAY

Sometimes the best deal you can set up for certain properties
is having renters stay there for free.

■ ■ ■

Over four decades, Hal Wilson has become one of the most successful and well-known real estate investors in Nashville, Tennessee. On at least two occasions, he has correctly anticipated hot investment areas and properly positioned his business and his associates as the areas started to warm. They have all reaped tremendous benefits from that insight. However, Hal laughingly admits he made a slight miscalculation on one of his investment properties in a not-too-hot area.

Hal had purchased a two-story, 1,800-square-foot house on North Second Street in east Nashville. He expected the neighborhood to rise quickly and steeply in value, just as the nearby neighborhood had. He paid $12,000 for the house and obtained a $30,000 loan— with a built-in cash cushion so that he could rehab it. As he finished the rehab, he tried to sell it, but no buyers came forward. Then he tried to rent it, but no renters came forward. He eventually lowered its rent to $400 a month and finally attracted renters. But within a few months of moving in, the tenants quit paying their rent.

Hal contacted the tenants and asked for the rent they owed. They said they were sorry but they just didn't have the rent money. Hal thought about the situation for a while. He had just fixed up the house and, with all of its new appliances and fixtures, it was one of the nicest homes in the neighborhood. He surmised that the neighbors would rob and destroy the house if the tenants moved out. The appliances, the new cabinets, the copper plumbing, the lights, the commodes, and all the other improvements that he'd made would be gone in an instant.

That's when Hal realized that the best decision was to keep the house occupied, so he told the tenants that they could stay without paying rent. With mock seriousness, he asked his tenants to let him know when they had some rent money.

After giving his tenants free rent for six months, Hal received a call and heard some seemingly miraculous news. His house that he'd rented for free had burned to the ground but, thank heavens, no one was hurt. He quickly called his insurance agent and asked if the house's policy was current. It was. The fire marshal later determined that one of the tenants' children had been playing with matches underneath the stairs and accidentally burned the house down. Hal didn't lose on this house after all.

4. CONSIDER RENT-TO-OWN FOR GOOD TENANTS

Sometimes you can help your tenants more than you—
or even they—know.

■ ■ ■

A young couple in O'Fallon, Illinois, were getting divorced. When they saw the "We Buy Houses Quick" sign, they immediately called the phone number posted on it. Investors Don and Joni Schaeffer answered the phone and quickly came over to inspect the house and make an offer.

It was a 1,400-square-foot, three-bedroom, one-bath house with a two-car attached garage. The house reeked of cigarette smoke, and the paint was dingy, but, otherwise, it was in good condition. The Schaeffers made an offer, and the divorcing couple quickly accepted it. The Schaeffers closed soon after. They hired professional painters to apply two coats of Kilz, to hide the smoke stains, and new paint in every room. The Schaeffers also refinished the bathtub for only $250—much cheaper than replacing it. They owed a total of $60,000 on the loan, and they advertised the property as rent-to-own at $85,000. In 1994, this was the biggest deal of their careers.

Within a month or so, an older couple called and expressed interest in buying the house. They looked at it carefully and said they wanted it, but they seemed certain that they couldn't qualify for a loan because they had declared bankruptcy within the last three years. However, because the man was a disabled Korean War veteran, he had a modest but guaranteed monthly income. The couple gave the Schaeffers a $3,000 deposit and made arrangements to rent the house with a three-year option to buy. At the end of those three years, the Schaeffers could happily tell the couple's lender that they had made every one of their payments early. They got a loan and bought the house from the Schaeffers.

Just a few years ago, when Don ran into them at Wal-Mart and addressed them by name, they were ecstatic. They said that the Schaeffers's rent-to-own generosity had helped them buy a house and fulfill their longtime marriage dream. Don drove by the house recently and saw the couple outside, happily enjoying their own front yard.

5. WHO MOVED IN?

Pay attention to background checks of prospective renters
and give back the deposit (if you have to) to get rid
of tenants who don't pay.

■ ■ ■

Ginny Pitts rented a three-bedroom duplex to an engaged couple with children. The man, a long-haul truck driver, was frequently away from home.

Everything went well for eight to ten months. Then the fiancée moved out. The truck driver asked if another woman could move in. Ginny said that would be fine, contingent on her verifying and approving the woman's tenant history.

A month later, the tenant living in the other side of the duplex called Ginny with a maintenance request and a complaint about "all the late-night noise" coming from next door. That tenant's rent was one month behind, and Ginny had already served an eviction notice, so she decided to investigate the complaint personally. She soon discovered that the new girlfriend had definitely moved in—with her family of six children! She also discovered that the fiancée had moved back in—with her teenage son.

Ginny interviewed the new woman, the mother of six. The woman spoke pleasantly and asked if she could just rent the apartment for her family. She offered to complete an application and give a deposit. Ginny asked typical screening questions and received typical responses. She, of course, had never been evicted and she, of course, had never been subjected to collections. Then Ginny ran background checks and discovered that the woman had been evicted three times. What's more, she was the subject of several collection actions.

Ginny immediately told everyone to move out, forfeiting the tenant's deposit as back rent. For days, everyone complained, but once she returned the deposit money, they finally vacated.

6. KEEP TENANTS AND PROPERTY MANAGERS ON THEIR TOES

Don't blindly trust your property manager; know your rights
as a landlord. For good measure, drop in on your property
for surprise inspections.

■ ■ ■

Sally Reynolds (a pseudonym) became a landlord as many people do: she had a house that she couldn't sell and, believing she had no other choice, decided to rent it out. She hired a highly reputable management company and was extremely happy with the situation for the first three years. "After all," she said, "I was building equity while someone else paid the mortgage. What could be better?"

Well, she did learn what could be worse. The property management company was a husband and wife team, with the husband doing most of the work. He was honest, fair, and helpful—a genuinely good guy. "But if you've heard the expression *opposites attract*, then you know where I'm headed with this. His wife, who began to slowly take over the operations of their management company, wasn't quite as aboveboard as him. I admit, because I'd had such a positive experience with them and trusted them completely, when little problems started to crop up, I really didn't suspect that there was anything to be concerned about." The problems included a new tenant being late with a payment, more repairs needed, and so on. "Because I lived thousands of miles away, I couldn't exactly pop over and check it out."

Then the whole situation went south. The newest tenant had been living in the home about eight months. He was a single man with no children and had rented this 2200-square-foot house in a family neighborhood located in a less-developed area of town. Around it are horse farms, barns, pastures—not exactly supporting the high life of a bachelor.

Then he gave notice and said that he'd be moving at the end of the lease. "Fair enough," Sally figured. "Four months is plenty of time for my wonderful property managers to find someone. And find someone they did! They charged me the usual fee for placing a renter and sent the notice that the security deposit was in their escrow account. Everything appeared on the up and up. But then, the rent was late for the first four months of the new lease.

"I contacted the management company and spoke with a lovely new secretary who was so new that she didn't know enough to lie to me about the situation. Had it not been for her, I never would have known just how badly I'd been duped.

"It turned out that this new tenant, along with her four kids (she had said there were three, but neighbors later told me that there were four), had left her husband and moved in with my previous tenant. Effectively, she and her brood moved in and ran my good tenant off. When he moved out, he forfeited his deposit for her and her children to be able to stay there.

"At that point, the management company that I trusted, that was supposed to represent *me,* had just switched teams. That may sound harsh, but consider this: they did not have her fill out an application; they did not run any credit check on her; they did not notify me of what was happening (neither when she and her kids invaded the property, nor when they stayed after running off a perfectly good tenant); and they acted as though she was a brand-new tenant, charging me a finder's fee.

"The whole thing was a fabrication. And then, when the rent checks were late, *really* late, they played it off like they were handling the situation. So I requested a copy of the new tenant's application and demanded to see her credit report. That's when it hit the fan. They told me that I wasn't entitled to that information, which a landlord is clearly entitled to! So, when I pushed the issue, they told me that they would no longer represent me.

"That really piqued my curiosity. I had my lawyer send them a written request for the information (application, credit report, etc.), which their lawyer informed the managers that they had to release to me. In the meantime, they got the tenant to fill out the necessary papers to cover their butts.

"Finally, they did forward the requested paperwork along with the security deposit and the finder's fee that they'd essentially stolen from me. I wound up having to evict the woman and her four kids. She left owing two months rent and being responsible for about $10,000 in repairs to the property. She and her ex-husband filed for bankruptcy just before dropping off of the planet, never to be heard from again.

"It was a painful and exhausting lesson, both economically and mentally, and one that I wouldn't wish on anyone," she says.

7. WHAT TO DO WHEN TENANTS' LIVES CHANGE

You can never really tell from their applications how tenants
will live in your property.

■ ■ ■

Rusty and Velma Edwards rented a small duplex to a young couple whose rental application was less than desirable. Their credit scores were poor, but the man did have a solid, stable employment history. They both declared that they were improving themselves. The Edwards decided to help them and rented their one-bedroom duplex to them.

Everything went well for nine to ten months, until the Edwards learned that the young man had been sent to jail. The young woman, now on her own, had trouble making rent that next month, so the Edwards were patient. The following month, the young woman made her rental payment on time. Later, the Edwards found out that the young woman had allowed a friend to move in. The friend, who apparently helped her pay the rent, was a prostitute.

The Edwards weren't really sure what to do. They had agreed to help the young couple, but only the young woman was there and responsible for the rent. Then, over time, the Edwards realized that she had started prostituting herself.

In December, when Rusty went over to the duplex to collect the next rent check, he noticed that she was really looking rough. There were signs of drug use and lots of foot traffic to the place. He warned her that he couldn't put up with illegal activities in his duplex. He went home to discuss the situation with Velma, and they started figuring out what they should do. It was winter, almost Christmas, and they really hated to put anyone out of a home that time of year. But soon after, they received a call from the young lady who said she was being physically and mentally abused.

Rusty went to the duplex, picked her up, and took her to a local shelter for abused women. A couple of days later, he stopped by the duplex and discovered that a pimp and several drug users were still using his duplex as a place to hang out. Rusty warned them that they should leave, and they left—but later came back. He then posted "No Trespassing" signs, but they ignored them and continued to hang out.

On the afternoon of December 24th, Rusty boarded up the duplex so that no one could get in. Several weeks later, the young woman came and picked up her few remaining items. The Edwards easily rented the duplex again, but this time they were more cautious. They learned that careful screening is important, yet landlords can never really know how their tenants will live in their properties—or how their lives may change.

8. REFERENCES MAY NOT BE WHAT THEY SEEM

Hire a professional to help you screen prospective tenants.
Private detectives and other professionals have training and
experience to obtain limited-access information for you.

■ ■ ■

Vicki Bianchi has been an active real estate investor since the late 1970s. Like any investor, she has seen her fair share of tenant troubles. During her local real estate investor group meeting several years ago, Vicki listened to a licensed private detective describe how her services could help landlords. The detective offered her clients a trained eye for detail and the ability to deliver individualized services at a reasonable rate.

For a fee of $19 for every Social Security number, the detective offered landlords a full tenant screening package, including calls to two previous landlords, one previous employer, one listed reference, and a family member *plus* the standard credit, criminal, and background checks. Vicki is an active investor, a trusted pharmacist, and a popular national speaker, so she decided to free up some of her time by hiring this detective. She has used her services many times over the years.

Several years ago, Vicki received a lease application from a prospective tenant and, without a thought, forwarded it to the detective. Within an hour, she called and asked Vicki if she'd noticed the suspicious phone numbers on the application. The prospective tenant had listed three similar numbers. According to the application, the current employer was at 555-3302, the current landlord was at 555-3304, and the personal reference was at 555-3307. She realized she was being toyed with, but with help from her detective, she didn't play along.

In another incident several years ago, Vicki received a mother-son lease application and, without a thought, forwarded it to the detective. Minutes later, the detective called to tell Vicki that she'd already received applications for this mother, son, and father from other landlords. She had already run a criminal report based on the first application and discovered that the parents were both convicted child molesters. The poor child was apparently stuck with them. A sad situation for sure but, thankfully, Vicki immediately had access to the definitive information she needed to make her rental decision.

9. MAKE SURE THE HEAT IS ON

Ask would-be tenants to show you proof that they have transferred utilities to their own account before you give them keys to the property.

■ ■ ■

Over the years, investor Vicki Bianchi has consistently rented her summerhouse to short-term tenants. Each of her last three summertime tenants has called her to complain about the cool nights and lack of heat. When she asked if they'd ordered that the natural gas utility be turned on, they all replied, "No."

That's why Vicki has learned to be proactive. She now reminds all of her tenants to transfer and turn on their utilities—and requests that they show her the paperwork to prove they did so—before she gives them keys to her rental property.

10. WHAT IF YOUR TENANT DISAPPEARS?

Collect and update the emergency contact information of
relatives from your tenants.

■ ■ ■

In the early 1990s, Don and Joni Schaeffer bought a 1,600-square-foot, two-bedroom, one-and-a-half-bath house in Belleville, Illinois, a suburb of St. Louis, Missouri. The Schaeffers rented the house as a Section 8 property to an elderly lady. She lived alone and she didn't seem to have any friends. But she was always friendly with the Schaeffers, and she usually paid her rent on time.

Her lone occasional visitor was her disabled grandson. When he visited, they kept to themselves and usually stayed inside the house. She required a walking cane and he always wore leg braces. Occasionally, she took short trips to visit distant relatives, but she always returned before long and paid her rent.

So, when she didn't send her rent on time, the Schaeffers assumed that she was away on one of her short trips. They waited a couple of weeks before trying to call her and her neighbors. No one had seen or heard from her for several weeks. Unfortunately, they didn't know the name or phone number of her grandson or any other relative. They didn't know what to do.

After three weeks of no communication, the Schaeffers entered her house with some trepidation. Her door was unlocked but no one was home. Don admits that he suspected foul play and somewhat anxiously opened closets and the refrigerator and the freezer in the basement. His heart was pounding, but he saw no blood, no body parts. Like a Wild West ghost town, everything in the house seemed to be in its proper place, but it all seemed so sterile. Then they noticed her dentures in a glass on her bed stand and someone's leg braces leaning against her bed.

Eventually, the Schaeffers moved all of her things into storage and sued for possession of the unit. They asked a relative who was a policeman to investigate her disappearance, but it still remains a mystery. To this day, Don half-heartedly jokes about alien abduction, because no one ever found out what happened to her.

11. THE MYSTERIOUSLY HIGH WATER BILL

Watch, wait, and listen for unusual clues about high usage
of utility services. The problem could be surprising and
the solution simple.

■ ■ ■

Investor/landlord John Ferguson (a pseudonym) in Nashville, Tennessee, responded to a call from his tenant about a $600 water bill. Even though he's not responsible for paying the water bill, he requested that the water company send an inspector out to check.

The inspector found no leaks in the plumbing system. None of them could figure out where all the water was going, and they stood in the hallway discussing the problem. While standing there, the tenant's dog trotted by and went into the bathroom, put its paw up on the toilet's flush lever, and pulled it. Then the dog sat and stared as the water swirled and swished down into the toilet—just as the tenant's money was doing. They thought, "Well, that's interesting." They waited for another ten minutes and observed as the dog returned, flushed, and watched the swirling water once more. After the third or fourth time, the landlord and the water company inspector turned to the tenant and said, "We think we know where your water is going—and you do have to pay your water bill." The tenant asked what she should do to keep the dog from flushing the toilet. "Keep the bathroom door closed," the inspector said. That solved the problem.

In retrospect, the landlord should have remembered some clues, because the same tenant had previously complained that her toilet was backing up. When he went over and snaked the drain, he couldn't make it go through a blockage. He removed the toilet from the floor and discovered a tennis ball wedged between the toilet and the drain hole in the floor. After watching the dog flush the toilet for amusement, it dawned on him: "Ah-ha. That's how the tennis ball got wedged."

12. THE CASE OF THE LEAKING TOILET

As a landlord, don't ever be shocked by unusual tenant behavior.

■ ■ ■

A tenant in Nashville started complaining to her landlord, Dennis Smith (a pseudonym), that the home's toilet was leaking. The landlord went over, inspected it, and determined that the leak was coming from the wax ring that seals the toilet to the floor. He removed the toilet and replaced the wax ring, and the toilet worked well for a week.

But then, the same tenant called to tell him the toilet was leaking again. He assumed he'd installed the wax ring improperly. When he went back, sure enough, he found the wax ring seal leaking. Again, he carefully replaced the wax ring seal and went home, confident that it would hold this time.

But one week later, he received another leaking toilet call from the tenant and returned to see that the wax ring seal was indeed leaking once more. He stood there, feeling puzzled, for quite a few minutes. While staring at the toilet, he mulled over his procedure and felt confident that he'd done everything right. Yet something was obviously wrong.

So this time, he asked the tenants if they'd noticed anything unusual—extra water pressure, perhaps. They hadn't noticed anything so, with reluctance, he carefully replaced the wax ring seal one more time.

Yet one week later, the same call came, and he returned to the culprit toilet. As he stared in disbelief, he again asked the tenants if they'd noticed anything unusual. A lightbulb clicked on this time when one tenant admitted he might have an idea what was happening.

As it turned out, these tenants were rather amorous and adventurous, and, well, they liked to make love on their toilet, although they quickly said they weren't sure if that could be the problem. The landlord urged them to understand that this lovemaking was most likely the problem and it would no longer be *his* problem. He agreed to replace the wax ring seal for a fourth time. From then on, the tenants would have to hire a plumber because, as he said, "Your use is not normal wear and tear."

His final wax ring seal is, as far as he knows, still intact on the toilet.

13. EVICTING DELINQUENT TENANTS

Use professionals to screen prospective tenants and avoid dire problems, especially when your rental property is far from home.

■ ■ ■

Early in their investment careers, Don and Joni Schaeffer bought a house in Alton, Illinois, more than 45 miles from their own home. The seller was a minister forced to move after his congregation split into two. He had leased the house for a while, but he wasn't happy being a landlord. Like most new landlords, when the Schaeffers bought the house, they fixed it up the way they would want it if they lived in it themselves—and eventually they did.

One day, as they finished rehabbing the house, a woman walked up and asked Don if she could rent the house. She told Don that she lived just down the street and that she was a widow with three kids. Her active-duty husband had recently been killed during a military training exercise at nearby Fort Leonardwood. She had no credit record because her husband had paid for everything, but she really needed a home. The Schaeffers called her references themselves rather than hiring a professional firm to do so. Her friends gave her glowing reviews, so they let her move in. Over the first six months, she made three payments that were late. Because she mailed her payments directly to the Schaeffers, she knew how far away they lived.

However, after the first six months, she stopped paying rent altogether, so the Schaeffers tried to evict her. Unfortunately, she never answered the door when they came by, so it took them six months to serve her notice successfully. They sued her for possession and for $550 a month in back rent. She answered their official complaint and demanded a jury trial. But because the county only conducted jury trials during two summer months, they had to wait. The delinquent renter got to stay in the home until the summertime court date arrived. The Schaeffers retained an attorney and kept him on standby when they made their court appearance. Their tenant failed to make an appearance, but the judge refused their request for summary judgment. Instead, the judge held a trial in absentia while the Schaeffers called and questioned witnesses—including themselves! After a 30-minute deliberation, the jury found in favor of the Schaeffers and the judge awarded them possession plus $6,000 for back rent and damages.

One month later, the sheriff evicted their tenant. When the Schaeffers entered their house, they found a complete disaster. Apparently, someone had lit a gasoline fire in the fireplace, and when some flames flashed back, that person had dropped the gas can on the carpet. The room had been badly damaged by fire. The Schaeffers needed an official fire report to make their insurance claim. When they called their local fire department, the operator thought that they were reporting a fire going on right then. After some questioning, they finally got through to the fire marshal's office. They had to arrange for the marshal to visit and make a fire report. After filing the claim, their insurance company paid for damages but then dropped their coverage. Because they couldn't obtain insurance coverage for a vacant house, the Schaeffers moved into this house—45 miles from their home—while they rehabbed and prepared to sell it.

It took the Schaeffers a full year to rehab and sell that house. They lost $28,000, but they finally sold it and moved back home. Six years after they sued their former tenant, she called and asked them to release their claim so that she could get a car loan. Don said he'd love to release the claim just as soon as she paid their $6,000 judgment (which she didn't do).

Over the years, he has renewed the judgment to keep it alive and he says that—as a matter of principle—he will continue to renew it until they get their money from her.

14. WHEN SHOULD YOU START EVICTING?

Listen to your own experience as well as to advice from successful investor/landlords.

■ ■ ■

Rusty Edwards has been a full-time general contractor for 20 years and, with his wife Velma, has been an investor/landlord for 6 years. The Edwards currently manage properties and deal with 26 tenants.

Over the years, Rusty has read and heard many times that, if the rent is due on the first of the month and late on the sixth, then the landlord should start the eviction process on the tenth. Yet he's also heard every reason under the sun why a tenant couldn't pay their rent this month. His experience has convinced him that, if he allowed 40 tenants to pay late, then 38 of them wouldn't pay at all.

Today, he faithfully heeds the advice he's received and always starts eviction proceedings on the tenth of the month.

15. COLLECTING ON BAD CHECKS

Be persistent about collecting rent on bad checks,
even when tenants threaten bankruptcy.

■ ■ ■

A tenant of Steve Jones (a pseudonym) moved out during the middle of the lease—and put a stop payment on his last rental check. When Steve asked him to make good on the check, he refused, so Steve took him to court and got a default judgment. Unfortunately he could not file a garnishment, because the man had recently graduated from school and was unemployed.

The tenant then appealed the court judgment through his attorney but didn't bother to show up for the hearing. Steve insisted on getting the money, and the tenant said that he could only afford to pay three cents on the dollar or he'd have to file bankruptcy. Steve replied, "Okay, file bankruptcy." The tenant told him that a bankruptcy would wipe out the judgment, but Steve said he'd prefer to have the tenant have a bankruptcy on his record than accept three cents on the dollar for his debt. He also knew that bankruptcy would cost the tenant significantly more in the long run.

What else had the tenant overlooked? That he had written a check for more than $1,000 and then placed a stop payment order on it—after having lived in the rental home. In Tennessee, it's a criminal offense to put a stop payment on a check for services after the services have been rendered. According to the law, the tenant could get a year in jail.

The tenant then told Steve that he had moved to North Carolina, which actually made his bad check a federal issue. The tenant could get five years in prison for that. Steve told him that he would process the bankruptcy notice but that, unless the tenant picked up the check balance and paid the attendant fees, he would have to notify the federal prosecutor of this situation. The tenant told him that he couldn't do that, because the debt would be wiped out by the bankruptcy. Steve told him that he was not trying to collect the debt; he was following the legal process required when someone writes a bad check.

So the tenant filed bankruptcy, and Steve filed notice with the federal prosecutor. This legal problem has gone on for almost three years. Yet for $2,500 and two stopped checks, the tenant is now running from the law and facing ten years in prison (five years for each bad check).

Most people think that they can threaten others and slink out of their debts. Steve believes that word gets around whether you are "soft" or "hard" on tenants, and he doesn't want to be known as a softie in his community.

16. THE DOWNSIDE OF PROPERTY MANAGEMENT FIRMS

Management companies will not manage your properties
as closely as you will. Only you will check all factors and
inspect your investment as often as necessary.

■ ■ ■

For many years, Rob Brown (a pseudonym) worked as a professional health care consultant. He was constantly on the road, never at home in Atlanta. He knew from family members and from his own engineer-minded research that getting into real estate was a great investment, but he was never home. He couldn't manage any investment properties—or so he thought.

In the midst of all his travels, Rob did manage to buy his own house. Then, still minded to acquire real estate, he found an investment deal that he couldn't refuse and bought his first rental house.

With this house, Rob really had his work cut out for him, and, for several months, he spent every weekend working on this new rental property. He knew he needed someone to manage the house for him. Some landlords manage their properties from "safe" distances, but Rob was convinced that Baltimore to Atlanta and similar distances were more than a bit too far. He looked around and asked for referrals to a reputable, ethical, and moral property management company, and he found it—so he thought.

The management company's principal was a real estate agent with 30 years of experience owning and managing investment properties for other investors. He was well liked in his community and an active church member, so Rob felt certain that he would do a fine job. Once he finished rehabbing the house, he turned his keys over to this manager and continued his travels.

Around Christmas during his first year working with this manager, Rob was invited over to his house for an evening of fine dining and entertainment with other investors. There, making small talk over dinner, Rob learned a great lesson. He asked the friendly, middle-aged man across the table if this manager also managed the properties he owned. The friendly investor man wisely and persuasively replied, "No. No one will manage my properties as well as I will, so I manage my own properties." Rob was a bit surprised, said thanks for the advice, and took it in stride. But still, he wondered. Rob believed that a professional management company had to be able to manage the properties better than he could, especially because he traveled so much. Besides, the manager gave Rob regular reports about his property and seemed to be keeping a close enough eye on it.

Over the next two years, Rob bought and submitted two more properties for the manager to take care of. He found some good deals and, with this management company, there seemed to be no real issues.

Actually, there *were* a few issues. When Rob returned home one weekend and opened his regular rental statement, he found a $25 charge against his rental income for "changing a lightbulb." Somewhat puzzled, he called the management company for an explanation. The manager couldn't take his call, so an assistant was kind enough to tell Rob that his tenant had complained about a lightbulb being out, so the management company had sent someone to change the lightbulb—for the standard visit fee of $25.

Rob was more than a little upset. He told the assistant that he saw no reason for the tenant to not change his own lightbulb and felt quite exasperated at the absurdity of it all. He hung up the phone.

Later, Rob contacted the management company to discuss getting some rehab work done on one of his rental houses. He asked for the manager, who unfortunately was not available. Luckily, however, the management company's property maintenance supervisor was available, so Rob talked with him and prioritized the necessary rehab work. One high priority item they discussed was roof repair. Large trees surrounded his rental house and, over the years, large branches— and even whole trees—had fallen on the roof and damaged it. Rob asked the property maintenance supervisor to obtain a repair estimate. Several days later, he called Rob with an estimate that seemed high. Because he had done some rehab and knew people in the construction business, he called around and got his own estimate.

As it turned out, the property maintenance supervisor's estimate was very high—about 150 percent more than the other estimates Rob received. So he went with the contractor that he knew whose estimate was much lower.

Over the next year or so, Rob noticed that the property maintenance supervisor's estimates were always about 150 percent of his own estimates. Naturally, he started to lose respect for the management company.

Although his travels still prevented him from undertaking day-to-day management activities, Rob tried to be a responsible landlord. He often drove by to check on his properties, and when he noticed or heard about something that needed to be done, he contacted the management company as soon as possible. While driving by his first rental house one evening, Rob saw two large dogs playing in the yard. He likes dogs but doesn't allow his tenants to have them. So, when he next spoke with someone at the management company—but not the seemingly always-busy manager—he mentioned that he had seen two large dogs in the yard. He asked the management company to investigate and enforce the terms of the lease, if necessary. When Rob next spoke with the management company, an assistant told him that they had investigated and determined that there were no dogs at his rental house. Still suspicious, Rob seriously started to consider not renewing his agreement with the management company.

Before long, the tenants moved out of Rob's first rental house. According to neighbors, the tenants kept two large dogs. These dogs had left a real mess in their wake. Apparently, while changing the lightbulb, the management company's representative had failed to notice the two dogs gnawing on doorframes and window frames and chewing holes through the drywall in several rooms. When Rob saw his first rental house after the family and dogs moved out, he immediately called the management company and told them that he would not be renewing their management agreement. Rob read them a laundry list of complaints that culminated with the dog carvings and declared he was done. Period.

In retrospect, Rob noted that the manager was always available whenever he stood to gain something. For example, when Rob bought a new investment property, the manager guided and supported his decisions in a personal way. When Rob restructured his investment business, the manager was available to collect his fees—er, to help Rob set things up properly.

As a constant traveler, Rob had needed someone to manage his investment properties properly, but now he looks back and feels much wiser. It seems that the friendly, middle-aged man that he'd met at dinner was right: no one manages investment properties as well as the owner.

17. HOW TO GET ACTION FROM LATE-PAYING TENANTS

Employ creative, effective ways to get the attention of
tenants who are delinquent in paying rent.

■ ■ ■

It's not surprising that, over four decades of property management and investing, Hal Wilson has had to evict a few tenants for not paying rent. He has been to court on too many lengthy dispossessory actions and, like many investors, has decided that he doesn't really like them. So Hal has developed an alternative method for getting tenants to pay up or suffer "eviction." Here's how he does it.

When one of his tenants stops making rent payments, Hal, like most investors, usually just contacts them (especially if they're new tenants) and asks them to pay. With most people, he just has to make a phone call and they immediately send the rent. If he hears a valid excuse, he shows patience and helpfulness. If he hears an invalid excuse—which typically comes from naïve tenants—then he clearly reminds them that they have to pay their rent in a timely manner. Otherwise, he explains, they will have an eviction on their record and they may have trouble renting from other landlords in the future. If the naïve tenants fail to heed his warning or if experienced tenants just don't pay, Hal employs his own creative remedy. In broad daylight, he drives over to the property and sticks one of his For Rent signs in the front yard.

As soon as the tenants spot his For Rent sign in "their" yard, they call Hal and say something like, "What's with the sign in my yard?" Hal then tells them he assumed they were moving. Their usual response is, "No, we're not moving." In answer to that, he usually says, "So, let me get this straight. You're not moving, and you're not paying rent? That doesn't go hand in hand. If you stay, you pay rent. If you don't pay rent, you move. When you move, I rent the place to somebody else. And that's exactly what I'm doing."

Sometimes, after Hal declares this as gospel truth, they say in a huff, "Well, then I'm moving!" and Hal replies, "Good, that saves me a lot of trouble." Usually, though, the tenants quickly pay the rent.

As Hal has found, this one action really grabs the attention of his tenants and gets the results he wants—without wasting a lot of words.

18. OFFER TENANTS UPGRADE FEATURES

Make additional money by charging extra for extras.

■ ■ ■

Jack Price (a pseudonym) offers optional upgrades with the basic units he rents. One of the upgrades, for example, is to include a clothes washer and dryer set for an extra $50 a month. Jack buys these sets for $300 through a local appliance salvage company, so he makes back his cost in just six months. Because most renters seem to want immediate gratification, they are likely to pay Jack for something they could easily buy more cheaply at a later date.

19. CODES AND RULES— FOR YOU AND AGAINST YOU

Know local tenant codes, and you'll be armed with the
information you need to protect your interests as a landlord.

■ ■ ■

A group of church officials had approached John Wilson (a
pseudonym), a Nashville landlord, saying they were sponsoring a
Hispanic family and would guarantee payment of rent in a duplex in
the owner/landlord's multiunit building. When he asked who would
be living in his apartment, they said, "Just the family's grandmother
and granddaughter."

Two weeks after the family moved in, their neighbors in the
building called him to say that 50 people were living in this two-
bedroom duplex. The tenants assured him not to worry, that their
family was just visiting and they'd be leaving soon. So, he returned
to his office, called the neighbors, and told them that the family of
50 would be gone within 10 days. "You won't have to put up with
the noise much longer."

Ten days later, the neighbors called and told him that the family
of 50 was still there. So John went back over to the apartment and
discovered that the original family members had, indeed, departed.
They had, in fact, moved to unit B, the people from unit B had moved
to unit C, and the people from unit C had moved to his unit. He quickly
discovered two things: (1) having close family quarters is common
in the Hispanic culture, and (2) local laws allowed family members
to visit for ten days—regardless of their numbers. As a landlord, he
couldn't get around that. He had to accept the fact that, once each
month, the same ten people would live for ten days in his unit.

Then he got smart and called his local rental codes department
for more information. He learned that the code requires 125 square

feet for a first adult resident, 100 square feet for each additional adult, and no square feet for children. This gave him a way to refuse to renew the lease. John was willing to tolerate the existing situation until the current lease expired, but the neighbors next door wouldn't. They left.

Learning that the neighboring unit was vacant, the problem family asked if they could rent it. John balked at first, but they countered by explaining that if he rented them an additional unit, he could reduce the wear and tear on his existing unit. With that in mind, he agreed to rent them the recently vacated unit for a term scheduled to end at the same time as their original unit lease. His condition was that they'd accept the unit as-is and not require him to clean it up. So they rented both units without incident until the first lease ended, then moved out.

Shortly after the Hispanic family left, though, John received a call from the new tenant of the second unit. Apparently he'd turned on the water tap, discovered there was no running water, and, lo and behold, found out there was no water meter! So John called the water company, saying someone must have stolen the water meter. However, the water company told him they'd actually removed the meter six months before because they thought someone was stealing water. They made that deduction based on their observation that someone was living in the unit but the water had never been turned "on." John investigated further and found out that the Hispanic family didn't want to pay a $35 water connection fee. Instead, they had run a garden hose from the outside faucet on the first unit to the outside faucet on the second unit, then turned off the water line to the second unit at the street. All their ingenuity saved them was the $35 connection fee, though, because the total bill for both was paid by those in the first unit.

How could he right the situation? John was told he'd have to go down to the water company, pay an installation fee, and sign a certification that he wasn't stealing water. Surprisingly, when he went there, he was told he'd actually have to appear in environmental court, because it was illegal to make his own connection without obtaining a building permit first. He told the water company, again, that he didn't make the connection and didn't even know about the connection until the violators had moved out and the new tenant had moved in. Regardless, the officials said he'd still have to appear in court and face a possible $500 fine.

Luckily, when John did show up in environmental court, the judge heard his case, immediately called it "absurd," and threw it out.

20. SECTION 8 RENTALS IN LOW-END NEIGHBORHOODS

People on public assistance for long periods can lose respect
for themselves and others, and they often don't keep
your property in good condition. Rather, they think that you,
the landlord, owe them something, so they constantly ask
for favors *and* don't pay their rent.

■ ■ ■

In the late 1950s, two partners bought an A-frame, four-family flat in Detroit near the assembly plant where Jeep Cherokees are produced. They owned the property until one partner sold out to the other in the late 1980s. For many of those years, the partners and their families lived in two of the units and rented out the other two.

Says Matt Fletcher, now a home inspector (http://www.miproperty .com) and the son of one of the partners, "My father decided to keep his interest in this fourplex for decades, believing that the rental income would be worth the trouble of being a landlord. He was correct—for a while. However, as the neighborhood got worse, so did the tenants. Every time someone asked him why he didn't sell the house, he'd say, 'That damn house paid for itself three or four times.

I'm keepin' it!' I think he just got attached to it because it was the first piece of property he ever owned."

Over time, this neighborhood decayed so much that only families on welfare would live there. Then the area got so bad that the owners could only rent rooms to men; families wouldn't live there. They became Section 8 rentals, which means that the government pays the rent for tenants on welfare. Comments Matt, "In reality, unless you want to be a full-time landlord and part-time social worker, I don't recommend renting to Section 8 tenants. Here's why. Whenever tenants would move out of a unit on Gray Street, my dad's property, they'd leave the unit in a filthy condition. I can remember one Section 8 tenant in particular. Roger didn't work often and was generally on welfare. Shortly after moving into the house, he said he found a chip of paint in the house and believed it was lead paint. He demanded that the paint be repaired so his children wouldn't eat it, resulting in brain damage. We fixed it immediately.

"Interestingly, Roger never talked to the landlords about the paint problem directly; we heard through the caseworker. In fact, he used the paint problem as an excuse to stop paying his rent. At that time, a Section 8 tenant had to specifically agree to have the check sent directly to the landlord. He had the government send him rent checks in his name and only paid rent to us when he felt like it, not when it was due.

"We knew there was no chipped paint in the house when he moved in. His children had likely chipped the paint off of the woodwork with a hammer and screwdriver. And when Roger moved, he left his trash and 'furniture' behind, he owed us money—he even left the water running in every sink and bathtub so we'd get stuck with a huge water bill.

"Roger was just one in a string of tenants like this. Sadly, even after cleaning up the house, these were the only kind of tenants we could attract because of the neighborhood."

After Roger and his family moved out, the owners started renting sleeping rooms in the fourplex. These tenants—divorced middle-aged and older men with drinking or drug problems—were actually better than Roger because they were clean and paid their rent most of the time. The landlords discovered that checking up on the place from time to time compelled the roomers to keep it in neat condition.

Yet the troubles never stopped. Says Matt, "My father's partner wasn't an honest person. My father had caught him charging for house repairs that never took place. Contractors wrote out receipts for work they didn't do. The partner would present the receipts to my father, explaining that he had already paid the contractors, so my father would give the partner half of the cost of the bill. But he's not a pushover. When my father discovered he'd been cheated, he went directly to his partner's house and demanded his money back, then and there.

"After nearly 30 years of ownership, my father finally sold his interest in this fourplex to his partner. A few months later, the house burned to the ground. No one was hurt, and the partner collected all the insurance money. The insurance on the house (replacement cost) exceeded the fair market value. I always thought that was quite a coincidence."

At least two more lessons can come out of this story:

1. Keep a close eye on partners because "people get funny when it comes to money."
2. Owning low-end property in poor neighborhoods means low profits and big trouble. Owning high-end property in good areas requires more money for acquisition, but profit margins are larger and headaches smaller. High-end property appreciates; low-end property does not (and might even go down in value). When you see a neighborhood begin to deteriorate, sell your property, even if you must take a loss. As Matt's father learned, it just isn't worthwhile to keep it.

21.   FIRE LEADS TO EXPLOSION BUT NO LAWSUIT

Try to prevent tenants from cutting corners and misusing
amenities that could spark costly accidents.

■ ■ ■

Salinas, California, has adopted an environmentally friendly
sanitation program. To reduce landfill waste and encourage recycling, residents may use one of three differently sized trash receptacles.
As you might expect, the smallest receptacle has the lowest fee, and
the largest receptacle has the largest fee. Unfortunately, if you produce more trash than your receptacle will hold in a given week, you
are stuck with it for an extra week.

Several years ago, Salinas investor Glen Marks leased his first
rental house, a nice two-bedroom, one-bathroom tract home, to a
tenant who decided to save money by paying for a smaller trash receptacle. Unfortunately, the tenant produced more trash than his receptacle would hold. After being stuck with extra trash for a while,
the tenant decided that he had to do something different. Rather than
pay for a larger receptacle, he decided to burn his extra trash.

He put the trash in the beautiful corner fireplace with a gas
starter. Glen explains what happened one night when his tenant
turned on the gas burner to light the garbage. "As he warmed himself in front of the fireplace, an explosion propelled him backward
about three feet. When we arrived at the house shortly afterward, the
firefighters, the county building inspector, and the gas and electric
guy were already waiting for us."

The explosion caused major damage to the fireplace and had even
lifted the corner of the house off its foundation. The tenant wasn't
hurt but was shaken up. Thankfully, he had opened the front door, so
most of the explosion's force dissipated through the opening. "I

thought we were going to get sued in addition to bearing the obvious cost of the damage."

The tenant didn't sue, though. In fact, he stayed in the house and kept paying rent while the repairs were completed—to the tune of $11,000. Contractors removed singed sheetrock, returned the displaced studs to the foundation, replaced sheetrock, and repainted walls. Shortly after the repair work was completed, the tenant lost his job, and he moved away a few months later.

Glen is happy that things worked out as well as they did. No one was seriously injured, and the property suffered no permanent damage or loss of value.

22. THE NECESSITY OF BACKGROUND CHECKS

Do extensive background and credit checks *before* giving keys
to tenants. Accept only cash or a cashier's check for
the deposit and first month's rent.

■ ■ ■

Investors and landlords Kathy and Glen Marks rented their three-bedroom, two-bath home to a couple and the husband's brother. The tenants gave Kathy a completed application and a $300 good faith deposit. Their references, although they checked out, were "different" from any others she'd experienced in her 16 years of managing rental property. Says Kathy, "The wife said her purse had been 'stolen' so she didn't have her checkbook, but she could give me a third-party check from a friend for the first month's rent and the balance of the deposit. The next week, the check bounced and the tenants were impossible to get a hold of. We learned that their previous landlord and employment references were bogus; they'd been carefully staged by cooperating friends. Our attorney also found out that they'd been evicted from their previous residence.

"So we started the eviction process and completed it two months later—just two weeks before Christmas. They were still in the house when the sheriff evicted them, Christmas decorations, tree, and all! By the time we were done, I felt like I had completed the Landlord/ Tenant Evictions 101 course."

23. DEALING WITH CULTURAL DIFFERENCES

Find fair and inexpensive ways to deal with cultural differences of renters.

■ ■ ■

People from some foreign countries often cook in large, family-sized pots. But American stovetop elements are not made to support 50-pound to 100-pound cookware, so Bill Benson (a pseudonym) had to replace electric elements on the stove at his rental home every 90 days or so. Before long, he decided that when he rents to cooking foreigners in the future, he won't include appliances in the units. Normally, if landlords furnish items such as appliances, they're responsible for maintaining them, although who's responsible for wear and tear is arguable.

To get around the problem of excessive occupancy, he stipulates in his lease that a two-bedroom unit allows two occupants for each bedroom in the basic rent; after that, it's an additional $150 per occupant per month. That way, he reasons, if renters have to pay for extra people, they'll rent extra units instead. If they don't, the wear and tear on a unit is high, so he collects money to cover it.

24. NO PLEASING HER, SO WHY TRY?

You can't please all your tenants all the time, and maybe you shouldn't try.

■ ■ ■

A woman wanted to rent John Sanders's (a pseudonym) 900-square-foot carriage house for only one week. He normally rents the suite for $1,250 a month on a yearly lease. He told her no, that economically he couldn't afford the cleanup expense for just one week's rent. She then asked if he'd rent for one month. Again, he told her no, saying his minimum rental time was a year. She asked if he doubled the rent to $2,500 a month, would he rent it to her for a month, or for three months, or for six months at that rate? He said no. Then she offered to rent it for $2,500 a month for six months and pay nothing for the last six months. That way, if she stayed for a year, she'd have paid her full rent, but if she stayed for less than a year, he would have made extra money. John said okay to that arrangement.

Checking her references, John found out that she didn't have a rental history, because she had moved into his unit from a house that she owned. Her parents had purchased the house for her, and she had lived in it two weeks before moving into a hotel. She moved out of the hotel because it was too noisy.

John should have been suspicious, because she said she couldn't sign the lease but that her attorney, a trustee, could. Because she came from a wealthy family, he figured that was no problem. But she certainly *became* a problem. She asked to paint the place purple: he said no, but she and her boyfriend painted it anyway. They let the paint drip and roll down the wall without smoothing it out, so runs of paint covered every wall and jammed all of the electrical outlets and switches. When she asked to replace the carpet, John said no because it was brand-new, but she got her boyfriend to install new carpet over the top of the existing one using a carpet steamer and adhesive. John discovered glue strips every four feet across his previously new carpet after she moved out.

Claiming she had a hearing problem, she turned off the refrigerator because she said it made too much noise. She also claimed that it wouldn't work. John turned it back on and discovered that all the knobs had been twisted and broken so that it couldn't be adjusted properly. When John replaced the refrigerator, she complained that it was too loud, but he put his foot down, saying it was the one provided with the lease.

Because the unit was older, John had completely torn out and rehabbed the interior just 18 months before she rented it, but she and her trustee complained that the new façade had hidden its age. She complained that there was "construction" going on in the attic when there wasn't any, then complained that the noise was caused by the fact that the place was old.

She also complained that the air conditioner wasn't working and claimed that her dogs needed the place to stay at 60 degrees. John sent the HVAC man to the unit and was told that his tenant was leaving the front door open so the dogs could go in and out easily.

In the end, she stayed for 18 months, paying $1,250 a month for the last six months. During that time, she was responsible for $9,000 worth of damage. To John's dismay, there was just no pleasing her.

25. HIGHER DEPOSIT HELPS PREQUALIFY TENANTS

Charge higher security deposits to cover cleaning costs
and prequalify tenants.

■ ■ ■

Joe Jackson (a pseudonym) requires security deposits equal to 110 percent of the monthly rent, explaining that the 10 percent covers hiring a professional cleaner to clean up after tenants vacate if they don't keep the place clean. If the prospective tenants protest, Joe assumes they will be messy and turns them down as renters.

26. ALLOWING PETS BRINGS IN MORE MONEY

You can make even more money from rental property
by allowing tenants to have pets.

■ ■ ■

Mike Mann (a pseudonym) allows his renters to have pets and charges a one-time, $500 fee for each. He has learned that responsible pet owners are willing to pay the fee—a premium for allowing pets—while those who are unwilling aren't as responsible, and he doesn't want them as renters.

He chooses not to charge a monthly pet rental fee, but he can charge higher rents because few landlords will allow pets. In the long run, he makes several hundred to several thousand dollars a year more than he would without his pet policy.

27. THE SEARCH FOR THE HOVERING STENCH

Never choose to overlook smelly situations—for the benefit
of your next tenants and yourself.

■ ■ ■

Lee Kerger in Atlanta, Georgia, bought a house that was in fairly good condition; it just needed some minor rehabbing. Or so it seemed, until he discovered a smell that wasn't going away. Specifically, Lee searched but could never seem to locate the source of a familiar but unidentifiable "animal smell."

Lee persevered and, eventually, with a few helpers, pulled up the ten-year-old living room carpet and discovered the source of the smell—animal feces. Piles of ten-year old animal feces and urine stains were spread over the underflooring and stuck to the underside of the carpet. For ten years, the carpet had lain there, and the stench had hovered almost that long, but apparently none of the several different owners had lifted the carpet and discovered the mess underneath (or they had found it and simply chosen to ignore it).

Lee discussed this horrendous surprise with several other landlords. They think it likely that subcontractors had been hired to lay carpet in the house but when they discovered the feces and urine, they didn't know what to do. Perhaps they couldn't get the occupant or owner to clean up the mess, or they'd been busy and decided to "get 'r done" as quickly as possible—ignoring the problem.

No one really knows how it happened, but Lee, determined to keep a smelly history from being perpetuated, took action and cleaned it up. Thank goodness for the next unsuspecting tenant!

28. DON'T NEGLECT EVICTION DUE PROCESS

Know the proper legal procedure to evict tenants
before you start an eviction.

■ ■ ■

Court Gettel has been an active real estate investor in Tucson, Arizona, since 1997. Court quickly moved into larger deals, and, for a few years, he owned and managed a 38-unit complex. Each 800-square-foot unit in the complex had two bedrooms and one bath. Each was furnished with kitchen appliances, including brand-new microwaves.

Like most diligent landlords, Court checks prospective tenants' credit scores and backgrounds. Like many landlords, Court has had some tenants with great credit scores and backgrounds skip out while still owing rent.

Several years ago, one couple stole the microwave furnished with the unit and moved out in the middle of the night while still owing $1,000 in rent. Because they were two months delinquent and he didn't want to take more of a loss, Court wanted to move quickly and rerent the apartment. As soon as he discovered that the couple had apparently abandoned their unit, Court told his on-site manager to change the locks and move all its nonfurnished contents into a storage unit. He also asked his attorney to start a formal eviction proceeding and file a suit for damages against the couple.

Within a week, Court had the defendants served with a formal notice that they had been evicted and that they were being sued for damages. Because the couple had been so derelict in their actions, Court assumed they wouldn't show up for their court hearing. And because his attorney had to appear at the hearing, Court decided to skip it and do other necessary work. In retrospect, he wishes he'd appeared at the hearing that day.

In his absence, the judge decided that the landlord had constructively and illegally evicted the couple from their apartment. It did not matter that the couple already owed him two months rent. It did not matter that the couple had stolen the microwave from their unit. What mattered, according to the judge, was that Court had not given the couple proper notice and had otherwise failed to follow legal procedure.

Court should have served the couple six days' notice that they were being evicted before he changed the locks on the door. Then, after properly serving the couple with six days' notice, he should have asked the judge to issue an eviction notice. Only then could he have the locks changed. The judge ordered Court to pay the couple $1,000 in punitive damages. Fortunately, Court later negotiated directly with the couple and was able to reduce his total damages payment to $100.

29. THE JOYS OF BEING A HANDS-ON LANDLORD

Be prepared to patch lots of problems from the ceiling on down.

■ ■ ■

Most real estate investors build their investment business with the sweat of their own brows and the strength of their own hands. Once they reach a certain level of success, the wise ones hire employees, independent contractors, and day laborers. Before they reach that level, though, most investors favor hands-on methods of patching problems around their properties. Hal Wilson had worked as a mechanic and a general contractor, so his experience prepared him to perpetuate the hands-on rule.

Several years ago, this investor from Nashville, Tennessee, had purchased a few houses on North Second Street in the east part of town. He had anticipated that the neighborhood would grow quickly but when it didn't, he was forced to keep rents low and maintain all of his rental properties himself.

On one occasion, Hal went to collect rent in person from a tenant who was several weeks behind. The tenant and his girlfriend were living in a two-bedroom, one-bath house, and they owed $300 a month. When Hal knocked on the front door, his tenant answered "madder than a devil" and told Hal, "You won't believe it . . . this place is falling apart . . . ." When Hal asked what he meant, his tenant explained in crude language, "We had that big rain storm on Saturday afternoon . . . my girlfriend and I was upstairs . . . and a slab of plaster fell out of the ceiling . . . it hit me on the butt!" He started laughing out loud, and Hal laughed along with his renter. Then he quickly patched the hole, repainted the ceiling, and collected his rent.

A few years later, Hal got a call from a different tenant in that same house. It was the dead of winter and the tenant told him that the water pipes had frozen and broken. Hal headed over to the property, and when he saw that the pipes were indeed broken, he got to work on them immediately. He opened the crawlspace door and crawled under the house. The broken pipes were far from the door where it was quite dark, so he kept his flashlight and his eyes trained straight ahead. When he finally reached them, he started trying to patch them. Because the pipes were made of galvanized steel, not copper, it was hard work and went very slowly.

As he tried to patch the pipes, he heard a high-pitched, leg-grinding, cricket-like sound getting louder and louder. So he stopped and waved the flashlight around a bit. He saw what must have been a hundred little beady eyes and grinding teeth. Rats.

Hal doubled the speed of his efforts and hurried out of there while the rats watched and waited. In fixing one problem, he'd uncovered another. Ah, such is the life of a hands-on landlord!

30. CRUCIAL STEP: CHECK APPLICANTS' CREDIT

Always run credit checks on tenants
before letting them move in.

■ ■ ■

Just four months before she was engaged and ten months before she got married, Terri O'Saile bought a beautiful new town house in a golf course community in the heart of Nashville, Tennessee. She had worked long and hard for her money, so she made sure she bought a place that had all the best features: three bedrooms, two-and-a-half baths, vaulted ceilings, a fireplace, a bar area, a utility room, and an attached garage and storage facility spread over 1,500 square feet. She paid $125,000 for this town house. After their engagement, Terri and her fiancé, Jason, decided they would live in his countryside house north of Nashville. Because Terri had recently purchased the town house, her best interest lay in using it as an investment and renting it out.

Terri tried for several months to rent her town house before she finally had an applicant who wanted to rent—and who said he wanted to eventually buy it. Her applicant appeared quite polished and spoke very well. Terri felt happy with her prospect, but she kept her wits about her—to begin with. She collected an application with background and credit report authorization clauses and an application fee. Then she checked her applicant's references and determined that he had a solid job with a large, reputable computer company. However, she didn't take the time to check his credit, because she had already moved in with Jason and her town house was costing her money to sit vacant. So she rented her town house to the applicant for $950 a month starting May 1, 2003.

Terri received timely payments until September 2003.

Then in September, as the first of the month dragged into the ninth of the month, Terri contacted her renter and asked him why she hadn't received his rent check. He apologized immediately and explained that he was waiting on money he expected from cashing in some employee stock options. Shortly after midmonth, the rent was finally paid.

In October and November, the same thing happened. His checks failed to show up, so she called him, he apologized, and she soon received his rent. However, in November, Terri learned from her renter that he had quit his job with his large, reputable employer to start his own business.

In December, his rent check again failed to show up. Her renter called on the ninth to say that he was having some short-term financial problems but that he was waiting on a large student loan, which would cover his December rent. That same month, Terri ran into her former next-door neighbor who told her that her renter had recently purchased a new luxury sport utility vehicle.

By January 5, the rent for December was still unpaid, and January's rent was past due. Finally, on January 23, both rent payments arrived.

February came and the rent was paid somewhat on time. Terri's renter assured her that his financial problems were behind him and that he would not have future problems.

In March, once again the first dragged into the fifth of the month without a rent check arriving. Terri contacted her renter, who told her that he had just hosted a seminar that day and would pay her when he received his money from the chamber of commerce in Arkansas. But by the end of the month, Terri still had not received his rent check.

By now it was April, and March and April's payments were both past due. When Terri contacted her renter again, they talked and planned to meet on April 13 to take care of the rent. When that day came, Terri made several calls to her renter. Those calls went unanswered for four days. On Saturday, April 17, her renter finally called. He stated that he had a court appearance on the morning of the 13, and, because of missed child support payments, the judge decided he should spend some time in the county jail. In addition, the money that he was to pay Terri for March and April's rent had gone to his ex-wife per the court order.

When Terri asked how he was going to make up for the past due rents, he told her that his sister was giving him the money. The renter's sister was in the process of buying a piece of property from the state of Arkansas. She was borrowing money to rehab the property and had enough equity to give her brother (Terri's tenant) rent money. Terri was able to contact the sister's lending institution representative, who stated that the loan had been approved but that a small amount of paperwork was still needed before the check could be released. This took place at the end of April.

Fortunately, Terri was able to continue to contact the lender for updates during the month of May and was told that, due to problems with the original title company, the lender was switching the loan to another title company. She was told that this would delay the check being issued.

In June, Terri again contacted the lender and was told that all of the paperwork had been received and that the lender's attorney was reviewing it for final approval. This also meant that once the attorney gave the green light, it would take less than 72 hours to release the check. By all accounts, it looked as if Terri's renter would be receiving the money from his sister within days. But, at the time this was written, she continues to wait and wait. While doing so, she uses her salary to pay her mortgage and her homeowner's association dues on time.

Looking back, Terri wonders if she did the right thing. She wanted to give her renter the benefit of the doubt, because he did state to her on occasion that he would travel to Arkansas to preach at his hometown church. Terri's renter is very grateful for her patience and hopes to have all rent monies paid in full to her by June 18. However, in Terri's mind, she sometimes fears that he may be taking advantage of her. On the other hand, she believes that he's a good person and that the situation will correct itself.

Though the rent was frequently late, Terri only once imposed the agreed-upon late fee of $25. If she were in this situation, would her landlord be as forgiving as she has been? She would hope so.

Still, she wonders about several things. She wonders why she didn't check his credit before she actually rented her town house to him—until she remembers how badly she wanted to rent her town house to cut her costs. Yet, as she wishes that she had checked his credit before she rented to him, she questions if the report would have shown anything bad. After all, he didn't quit his job until after he had rented her town house.

In the end, Terri feels burned by this first investment experience, and, honestly, she just wants out. Town houses in her community have appreciated to $130,000—$5,000 more than she paid—but mostly she wants out. She wants only enough to pay off her loan balance and offset some expenses. If someone offered her $123,000, she'd take it . . . but this time, she'd no doubt check the buyer's financial qualifications first.

31. SHORT-TERM DISASTER, LONG-TERM GAIN

Don't let bad experiences with tenants undermine the value of real estate investing over the long run.

■ ■ ■

In 1992, Dave Altman was working in Atlanta and got laid off from his job. He soon found work in Memphis, Tennessee, and had only two weeks to report to his new employer. He couldn't sell his house in Kennesaw, Georgia, that quickly, so he found a couple to rent the home.

Their credit and employment checked out, and everything looked fine. For five months, the rent checks arrived at Dave's place on time, then suddenly . . . no check. Says Dave, "It first happened during a holiday weekend so I wasn't overly concerned. But after several more days went by, I became very concerned." He made a telephone call to the tenants' home number and was greeted by a recording that stated, "The line is being checked for trouble." This typically means one of two things: a major outage has happened *or* the line has been "temporarily" disconnected for nonpayment.

So he made a call to the stock brokerage firm where the tenant said he worked. The phone was answered by someone who only wanted to know Dave's account information and if he could help him with his stock. But the tenant wasn't there. So he called the wife's place of employment at the tourism board. He was told that, "She ran off to England with her boyfriend."

Panic started to set in. "A call to the guy's brother resulted in finding out he'd been busted for dealing drugs and was in jail. A call to the next-door neighbor really alarmed me. He said he'd look at the house and would call me right back. On the return call, he emphatically told me to drive over there this weekend."

Dave arrived in his former neighborhood early Saturday morning and found his place literally destroyed. He recalls, "Even though a no pet policy was stipulated in the rental agreement, two large dogs had been locked inside for days at a time, judging from the amount of feces I saw. Someone had started a wood fire in the gas fireplace with ceramic logs and soot was everywhere. Everything of any value was gone. Not just the washer and dryer, stove, refrigerator, dishwasher, disposal, and sink—they even took the HVAC unit, the electrical panel, a lot of copper wire, the water heater with any easily available copper pipe, vanities, mirrors, and toilets. The bathtubs were left behind but heavily damaged. Anything of any value was either gone or damaged."

Dave continues, "The water bed had been drained on the floor. This was a three-story house, and the bedroom was on the second floor, so the first floor was a real mess—ceiling falling down, drywall falling apart.

"There were holes in the walls that had all the appearance of having someone's face shoved through the drywall, as well as lots of fist-sized holes. There were broken windows, ripped carpets. They had either one heck of a party or a seriously bad fight.

"Trash was everywhere. I stared at a real dump not fit for human habitation."

When Dave called his insurance agent, he was told that his homeowner's policy didn't cover renting the property to anyone, so any claim would be denied. "What could I do? I wound up signing it back to the mortgage company and taking a huge credit hit that lasted years.

"For years, I swore that I would never have renters again, but after reading *Rich Dad, Poor Dad* and playing the CASHFLOW 101 board game, I've started being a landlord again. Why? Because the returns are better than a savings account and more secure than my dismal 401(k). Plus, I'm not getting any younger. I do not expect the government to take care of me in my old age; they are just trying to take me for all I'm worth.

"I'll stick with real estate investing. It gives me some control over my future."

32. HEAD-ON COLLISION WITH REALITY

Warning to first-time investors: your tenants have radically different goals than you do.

■ ■ ■

This story comes from Rosemary Fuller Thornton, author of *The Reality of Real Estate* and *The Homes That Sears Built*. It's reproduced here with her blessing and in her words, as published in *The Reality of Real Estate*.

October 1984. I was sitting in an attorney's office, waiting for closing to take place on my very first well-selected, income-producing real estate investment. I was buying my very first apartment—my first rental property. It was such an exciting day. This was to be the very beginning, the tip of the financial empire I was preparing to build. Unlike armchair investors, who talked a great game and never did anything, I had taken that all-important first step. I was going to be a landlord. And, better yet, I was going to be a *wealthy* landlord.

I knew I was going to be a wealthy landlord because I was a well-educated investor. I had attended many, many seminars that offered all the secrets to financial independence through real estate. I had read all the books, listened to all the tapes, and, better yet, I had been a Realtor for several months. I knew everything I needed to know. Or so I thought.

We had found our investment property from an ad in the paper. The current owners were asking $69,500 for the fourplex, which had four one-bedroom units, each with a dining room, living room, kitchen, and bath. The top half of the building was asbestos shingle, and the bottom half was solid brick. It had been rerooofed by "Laurel and Hardy Roofing Company" two years earlier, and the owner told me the building was in "fair" shape.

Fair? What a misleading term. Fair maidens are lovely young ladies. Fair business dealings mean everyone is left happy. But a building described as being in "fair" condition is usually being sold for land value only.

The financing sounded perfect.

Cash down payment	$18,500
Assume onwer-financed first mortgage	45,000 (payments $509)
Assume owner-financed second mortgage	6,000 (payments $82)
Asking price	$69,500

The seller was a smart cookie and had everything all set for some poor sap to walk in, pay $18,500 down, and assume these two mortgages with no qualifying, no hassles, and a quick closing.

Enter poor sap.

We had obtained the $18,000 cash down payment by taking out a second mortgage on our own home. The monthly payments on the newly created second mortgage on our own home were $267. This, added to the apartment mortgages of $509 plus $82 ($591), came to $853. The rental income was $975, leaving us a positive cash flow of $117 a month.

It all looked so great on paper. We felt this property was the investment for which we had spent the last 12 months searching. The condition of the property was restorable, the price was fantastic, and the financing was excellent.

Closing went well, and, for the rest of the evening, my husband Tommy and I talked about what a good decision we'd made and how fortunate we were to be living out our life's dreams.

Part of our grand plan to transform this "fair" building from an eyesore to a mansion involved doing a bit of yard work. The first Saturday after closing, we arose bright and early, loaded 45,987 yard tools in our Toyota, and drove to *The Apartment.*

We'd not been there more than ten minutes when our first tenant approached us and introduced himself. Very proudly, I introduced myself as *The New Owner of The Building.* I had every reason to be happy. It was the 27th of the month, and I had no doubt this man had left the shelter of his home to thrust large sums of money in *my* hands. After which three more tenants would follow his example. It was time to collect rent. Imagine—in just a few moments, I'd be $975 richer.

But as I waited, I saw no money coming. I did not see this man make any motions suggesting money was close at hand. Taking a good look at this guy, I realized that it didn't look like he had enough money to buy some free advice. And he didn't. He told us he was going to be "a little late" this month with the rent. "What is a little late?" I asked, hoping against hope we were talking about a day or two.

"Well, I get paid on the 15th, and I can pay you then," he replied. Wouldn't you know it—I had the only tenant in the state of Virginia that got paid only once a month. Feeling awfully disappointed, I reminded him of the late fee and went back to killing weeds.

Barely ten minutes had passed before Tenant #2 appeared and announced that her gas stove had not worked since sometime around the turn of the century. She spoke of how close Thanksgiving was and related the sad story of how much her son wanted only one thing in this world, and that was a fine turkey dinner for Thanksgiving. She had told him, "Only if those new landlords will buy us a stove, so I can cook that fine turkey dinner for you."

Well, there were not many ways to respond to such a request. We could either say, "Why, certainly a new stove is no problem; we'd be pleased and honored to help fulfill your small child's precious and heartfelt wish for a home-cooked Thanksgiving dinner." Or, we could say, "What? A new *stove*? Just so you and your boy can *eat*? No! No! *NO!!* Now get out of here and stop pestering me! I need to count my money—"

We told her that if we could not repair the old stove, we'd replace it with a better one. (*Better*—landlord lingo for slightly used.)

Tenant #2 then volunteered the information that she'd have her rent "sometime around the first." *Around* is another one of those words that has one meaning in the real world and another meaning when used to describe when rent will be paid. *Around the first* should mean before the first, on the first, or after the first. But when tenants tell you they will be paying their rent "around the first," it always means *after* the first. The $64,000 question is how many days, weeks, or months after the first we're talking about.

But now, a promise of rent was all we had to look forward to. We went back to work, pulling weeds, clipping bushes, and edging curbs but with rapidly dwindling enthusiasm.

Only seconds passed before Tenant #3's shadow darkened our work area. She was a normal-looking young girl, even well dressed. We were fairly surprised to hear she lived in our apartment. She also did not have large sums of money to stuff in our hands, but she did have complaints. All of the electrical outlets and light switches in her living room and dining room were broken, and when she had told the former owner about this little dilemma, he had told her to "just let the new landlords know." Hmm.

And last but not least, Tenant #4 showed up. By this time, we simply asked, "What is *your* problem?" while still harboring a glimmer of hope that she had come out to pay us our rent money. (Something we'd thought about a lot more than any of our tenants had.) It seems her furnace (a gas space heater) didn't look right. Not that it didn't work right, but that it didn't look right. It seems she hadn't had the gas turned on yet because she owed the gas company several thousand dollars from a previous address, and they wanted her to pay the old bill plus a substantial security deposit before they would reconnect. Picky people. Smart people.

We ventured upstairs and took a look at her space heater. Tenant #4 was right. This space heater did not look right. It didn't even look like a space heater. The number of parts in the heater that were still upright, unbent, and intact was fewer than four. She'd told the former landlord about her space heater, and he had told her, "Just let the new landlords know." In the meantime, Tenant #4 had been using her electric range to heat the apartment, burning out the elements on top one by one.

What we did not know, but would soon learn, is that no one in Virginia or neighboring states sells space heaters. But maybe we could find one used. Slightly used. And find a stove for the little boy's Thanksgiving turkey, and wait until the 15th for the rent, and see what *around the first* really meant, and hire an electrician at $500 an hour to find out why apartment #3 had no lights.

By now, the importance of yanking dandelions from the building's lawn had fallen a few notches on our priority list. Doing yard work at 1248 Decatur Street was now item 6,859 of "relatively unimportant things to think about doing before I die." In these last 60 minutes, we'd learned more about being a landlord and rental property owner than we'd learned in 12 months of reading and studying books about real estate investing.

Disheartened and disappointed, we threw our tools back in the car, yelled at our two little girls to hurry up, hopped in the car, and took off. Our grandiose vision of tenants handing us thousands of dollars each and every month in a prompt and timely manner was now just another fantasy that had no basis in reality. Suddenly, the harsh realities were destroying the pleasant thoughts and hope-filled dreams we'd cherished for so long. It was time to go home, reread some of those books, and ponder the situation. Tomorrow would be a better day.

■ TIPS

1. Your best deals could be the ones you *don't* do.

2. Be a good listener—you never know where your next tenant will come from.

3. Sometimes the best deal you can set up for certain properties is having renters stay there for free.

4. Sometimes you can help your tenants more than you—or even they—know.

5. Pay attention to background checks of prospective renters and give back the deposit (if you have to) to get rid of tenants who don't pay.

6. Don't blindly trust your property manager, and know your rights as a landlord. For good measure, drop in on your property for surprise inspections.

7. You can never really tell from their applications how tenants will live in your property.

8. Hire a professional to help you screen prospective tenants. Private detectives and other professionals have training and experience to obtain limited-access information for you.

9. Ask would-be tenants to show you proof that they have transferred utilities to their own account before you give them keys to the property you're renting to them.

10. Collect and update the emergency contact information of relatives from your tenants.

11. Watch, wait, and listen for unusual clues about high usage of utility services. The problem could be surprising and the solution simple.

12. As a landlord, don't ever be shocked by unusual tenant behavior.

13. Use professionals to screen prospective tenants and avoid dire problems, especially when your rental property is far from home.

14. Listen to your own experience as well as to advice from successful investor/landlords.

15. Be persistent about collecting rent on bad checks, even when tenants threaten bankruptcy.

16. Management companies will not manage your properties as closely as you will. Only you will check all factors and inspect your investment as often as necessary.

17. Employ creative and effective ways to get the attention of tenants who are delinquent in paying their rents.

18. Make additional money by charging extra for extras.

19. Know local tenant codes and you'll be armed with information you need to protect your interests as a landlord.

20. People on public assistance for long periods can lose respect for themselves and others, and often don't keep your property in good condition. Rather, they think you, the landlord, owe them something, so they constantly ask for favors and don't pay their rent.

21. Try to prevent tenants from cutting corners and misusing amenities that could spark costly accidents.

22. Do extensive background and credit checks before giving keys to tenants. Accept only cash or a cashier's check for the deposit and first month's rent.

23. Find fair and inexpensive ways to deal with cultural differences of renters.

24. You can't please all your tenants all the time . . . and maybe you shouldn't try.

25. Charge higher security deposits to cover cleaning costs and pre-qualify tenants.

26. You can make even more money from rental property by allowing tenants to have pets.

27. Never choose to overlook smelly situations—for the benefit of you and your next tenants.

28. Know the proper legal procedure to evict tenants before you start doing it.

29. Be prepared to patch lots of problems from the ceiling on down.

30. Always run credit checks on tenants before letting them move in.

31. Don't let bad experiences with tenants undermine the value of real estate investing in the long run.

32. Warning to first-time investors: Your tenants have radically different goals than you do.

PART 2

FINDING GOOD INVESTMENT DEALS

■ ■ ■

According to the law of scarcity, good investment deals should be scarce. According to the successful real estate investors whose stories are featured in this book, good investment deals are out there, but sometimes you may have to look hard for them.

More than anything, real estate investors suggest that finding good investment deals is just a numbers game. One common investing adage says that, on average, if you look at 100 investment deals, you will find 10 that are worth an offer, and 1 will actually work out for you. So if you want to find good investment deals, you have to find a lot of deals. Period.

Many successful real estate investors regularly stumble onto new, unusual deals. If you want to be successful, you should welcome new and very different opportunities for deals, as several of the following stories portray. Learn every way that you can buy, sell, or lease complete or partial ownership of a piece of real estate. Some successful real estate investors never even go inside their investment properties. Those investors make just as much money as others merely by doing paper transactions with loans and tax certificates. Understand that different types of real estate deals work for different types of real estate in different situations. Learn about different types of real estate deals so that you can be ready for the newest, most unusual situation at hand.

Many successful real estate investors no longer have to search for interesting real estate deals; other people bring interesting deals to them. Indeed, every real estate investor would like to have lucrative deals delivered to them on a regular basis. To be a successful real estate investor, you need to cultivate connections everywhere. Cultivating relationships also means rewarding everyone who brings you good real estate deals.

As you start investing, you may have to call everyone, drive everywhere, attend every possible public sale, read every classified ad, and do everything possible to make yourself known. When you start closing deals, be sure to reward everyone who helped you with them. It's a simple law of life: If you take care of those who help you make the deals happen, they and others will bring you more deals.

Successful real estate investors also know when to sell their investments. Sellers must make many of the same considerations that buyers do. To analyze a sales deal, for example, you need to estimate any fix-up costs and transaction expenses you'd have to pay to close the deal. You should also find comparable sales prices for your real estate. Once you gather your estimates and determine a comparable sales price, then you can decide how much profit you want on the sale and set your actual selling price. Because everyone wants a deal, buyers will seldom pay your stated price. So, once you negotiate a final sales price with your prospective buyer, you need to verify that this buyer has adequate funds before you sign a binding purchase and sales contract. Alternatively, you could sign a purchase and sales contract and include the contingency that it only becomes binding if the buyer proves to have adequate funds within a certain time frame. If you can't find a cash buyer and really want to sell a property quickly, you could consider offering seller-financing to a qualified buyer.

Sometimes, the smartest thing you can do is find one geographic area and concentrate on farming it—which means learning the territory inside and out. Once you know everything about that locale, you will spot patterns and anticipate cycles. For example, chances are that, while one neighborhood is hot, another is heating up, and another is already warming. That's because the longer you invest, the more you realize this truth: like so much of life, good investment deals come in cycles.

Sometimes you don't have to do much except just be in the right cycle at the right time. You can get really lucky, and sometimes, by tapping into your insights and being persistent, you even make your own luck.

33.   HIDDEN SIGNS, HIDDEN DEALS

Keep your eyes open for For Sale by Owner signs that
can't be seen easily.

■ ■ ■

From time to time, property owners feel hesitant about deciding to put their property up for sale and half-heartedly post a For
Sale by Owner sign in an obscure corner of the lot. Because they
aren't sure about wanting to sell, they haven't contacted real estate
agents and gone through multiple listing services. Not surprisingly,
small signs placed awkwardly tend to disappear from sight as grass
and weeds grow up around them. Even people who frequently pass
by rarely spot these signs.

But investor Barbara Downing has eagle eyes. Cruising around
an area of Atlanta, looking for deals, she drove by one property and
spotted a For Sale by Owner sign that had been placed at an odd
angle on a corner of the lot a year before. She contacted the homeowner and, within days, had put the house under contract. She succeeded in purchasing this property—a three-bedroom, two-bathroom
house with basement on five-and-a-half acres. It also had a four-stall
horse barn, a riding ring, a fenced pasture, and a creek and woods
nearby. For all this, she closed the deal for $170,000.

Just after putting the house under contract, Barbara placed a
"Real Estate for Sale" ad in her local newspaper. Within days, she
resold the $170,000 property for $190,000. Ironically, the buyer
lived less than a mile from this choice property. He had driven by it
daily for over a year and was so familiar with it, he bought it from
Barbara without asking for an inspection. When the original homeowner asked Barbara how she sold his home so quickly, Barbara
spared his feelings and said that she made sales like this all the time
because she just knew how to market houses. The truth was that the

buyer who had driven by that property daily for more than a year never did see the For Sale by Owner sign hidden by the overgrown weeds and grass.

34. LOOKING AROUND PAYS OFF

Research local real estate regulations and know property values
in the area you want to invest in.

■ ■ ■

Barbara Downing had located four lakefront lots that she was interested in buying—but none of them had boat docks, which she knew prospective buyers would demand. So Barbara met with officials from the Army Corps of Engineers, and they approved two single-slip docks for the two lots.

At that point, she contacted the owners of these lakefront lots and offered them $69,900 for all four lots. She offered to put down $600 in earnest money and would close within 60 days.

As soon as the owners accepted her offer, Barbara advertised the lake lots for sale in the local newspaper and quickly found a buyer for two of them. At a back-to-back closing, she sold two of the lots and walked away with a $5,000 profit *and* the two remaining lakefront lots. She sold them within four months for $55,000 and $60,000 each. Her total out-of-pocket cost was $600—not bad for a day's work.

35. INVESTMENT CRUISING

You can reap dozens of personal and professional rewards
by attending a National Real Estate Investors Association
(NREIA) cruise.

■ ■ ■

After joining and attending only two meetings of the Baltimore chapter of the National Real Estate Investors Association (NREIA), real estate agent Maureen Bream and her husband, Bob, signed up for a 2004 National REIA cruise. Maureen and Bob hoped they could learn from the experts and the program, capitalize on valuable networking opportunities, and make new friends who were also involved in real estate investment. In the worst case, they figured, they would simply enjoy cruising to new and exotic destinations.

Maureen and Bob wasted no time making their expectations come true. Before they even boarded their plane to leave Baltimore, they met another couple in the airport terminal reading the NREIA cruise booklet and launched a conversation with them. The two couples quickly became friends.

Every day on the cruise, Maureen and Bob learned more about real estate investing and networked with new people. Before the cruise, when they talked with noninvestors, they usually heard discouraging words like, "Oh, you can't do that." On the cruise, though, everyone seemed to have a can-do attitude. They heard people saying, "I can help you with that . . . here's my card . . . give me a call." Everyone welcomed their questions and assured them that no question they could ask would be considered "stupid."

Their days at sea were packed with knowledgeable and dynamic speakers who had been there, done that. Evening discussions offered them opportunities to chat with one another and quiz the experts during informal question-and-answer sessions. They switched dining companions at each dinner, so even mealtime became another learning and networking opportunity.

Maureen and Bob admittedly felt nervous and intimidated when they signed up for the cruise. Looking back, however, they have no regrets. They made many new friends, learned as much about real estate as they could in six days, and—oops, we almost forget to mention—they visited three Caribbean islands. (These cruises are offered several times a year. For information, go to http://www.nationalreia .com.)

36. MOTIVATION FIRST, LOCATION SECOND

It's never about the property; it's always about the motivation of the seller.

■ ■ ■

It's commonly said that the most critical thing investors should be concerned about is the property itself—its condition and location. Investor and author David Finkel (http://www.resultsnow.com) says the truth is that both of these considerations come second to one other factor: the motivation of the seller. If the seller is not motivated, then no matter what the condition or the location of the property, you still won't land a great deal. But if you work with a motivated seller, then you have a great chance of turning a handsome profit no matter what the property's condition or location.

Says David, "When this concept really sinks in, it can revolutionize how you prioritize your search for finding great deals. No longer do you waste time doing due diligence and inspecting the house until you've made sure you've found a motivated seller. Finding this motivated seller becomes the most important activity you can ever engage in. That's what you must focus your time, efforts, and creativity on."

37.   KNOW THE PROPERTY'S HISTORY

If you know the full history of a property, you can enhance both your confidence and your position during a buying transaction.

■ ■ ■

Dan Auito, investor and author of *Magic Bullets in Real Estate* (http://www.magicbullets.com), says that well before they make an offer, investors can begin to research history and succession of ownership through county records and tax rolls and by contacting previous owners as far back as possible. Optimally, the search ends by contacting the original owner and builder of the property.

38.   BAILING AN OWNER OUT OF A TOUGH SITUATION

Sometimes you can get a fantastic buy simply by honestly helping someone who is having tough times.

■ ■ ■

Judy Cook used to live in a subdivision and was interested in finding a property that had more space. She wanted to buy a quarter horse and looked into stabling a horse, but she quickly learned that it would be quite expensive. She says, "Still, I liked the idea of living in the country. With a lot of persistence, I found a house that the owner felt shy about selling. She had lots of problems to deal with. Her husband had built an airplane and stored it in the barn on their property. Unfortunately, when he flew that airplane on a test run, the plane blew up with him in it. I don't know that they ever did find the remains of his body."

His wife, Kathy, not knowing what to do and never having managed the couple's finances, decided to move herself and her two young sons into the city. This four-acre property with its Quaker-style barn and rambling, one-story farmhouse was simply too much to take care of herself.

This happened when the price of real estate was very low, so a real estate agent convinced Kathy that she'd be better off renting out this property rather than selling it. Indeed, the agent believed that he, too, could make as much money renting it from time to time as he could by selling it. Renting certainly would provide a solution for Kathy, especially because big houses weren't readily selling that year.

This went in Judy's favor. She recalls, "I asked around about the history of this property after I first became interested in it. When I talked to the neighbors, they told me that, for a while, they saw cars going into the barn but didn't see them coming out. Eventually the sheriff's department was alerted to that activity. It turned out that the barn was being used as a chop shop: people were stealing cars, cutting them up, and selling the parts. Before long, those people went to jail, and the house became empty again."

After that, Kathy had instructed the real estate agent to rent it again, saying, "But be sure the people you rent it to don't have tools. I don't want this to happen one more time." The agent found another family to rent it. These people had no tools whatsoever; they paid their rent on time; they seemed to live there happily for quite a while—until one day they reported that the furnace wasn't working correctly. So Kathy called a local furnace repair shop owned by a friend of hers. A repairman went to the house, walked up into the attic via the staircase, then quickly came back down the stairs, got in his car, and drove eight miles to the nearest pay phone. He called Kathy from the pay phone and said he wasn't going to fix the furnace, not in that property. "I wouldn't dare be caught there," he told her. He had found stashes of money in the attic, right by the furnace, and the people living there were cutting some kind of white powder on the butcher-block island in the kitchen.

This family got ousted from the property, and Kathy, bitten twice, was afraid to rent it again. So she told her oldest son, now old enough to live in the house by himself, to stay there and take care of the property until she could sell it. The real estate agent put signs in the front yard, but the son kept taking them down and putting them in the barn. Guess what? He had the greatest hangout you could imagine: a huge, sprawling, four-bedroom home with 34-foot ceilings in the living room, dining room, and den; a double-faced stone fireplace; a kitchen to die for; a huge utility room and office; and a Quaker-style barn—all on four acres with a corral and pasture land. Why would he want to give this up? This place had become his chick magnet!

Judy continues, "Then I came along to possibly buy this property. I found that the young man had changed all the locks, so no real estate agent could get in. But after looking through the windows of the home, we deciphered that it was probably an excellent buy—if we could just see the inside.

"So I went to my car and took out a sledgehammer. (I was ready to pay for replacing a window if it meant finding a great deal.) Once the sledgehammer came into view, the young man inside quickly opened the door.

"Once I was able to tour inside the home, it was easy to make a good offer. Our offer sounded like this:

> We would like to rent the property with the option to purchase it at the end of 12 months. During that 12 months, we'll rent it at the same price the previous tenants had paid. At the end of the 12 months, we have a set selling price, and should we not buy at the end of that 12 months, we will pay a different (higher) sales price at the end of 24 months. Then, at the end of 36 months, the price would go up again. (Note: According to the agreement, the rent itself wouldn't go up, only the price of the house.)

"We realized that it needed a lot of repairs, so we negotiated that the rent would be what the other people had paid, minus $300 a month for repairs. We agreed to send Kathy a check for any remaining funds left over from the $300 and include receipts for the repairs we paid for from this money each month.

"You can see that, with this arrangement, we weren't paying much rent overall. Even though the market had gone up, our rent stayed the same as what the previous tenants had paid. We were spending $300 a month on improving a property that we were going to own in the future. Just think of the consequences.

"When we presented our offer to Kathy, her only questions were: 'Do the buyers have a criminal background? Have they ever been arrested on criminal drug charges?' The answers to her questions were no, and to prove it, we even paid for a criminal background check, which went directly to her.

"All of this happened to our benefit, because we were willing to take a chance on that house, see through the mess, and help out a distressed owner."

39. WHY NETWORKING CONTACTS ARE CRUCIAL

Build a networking team, and show appreciation when team members come through for you.

■ ■ ■

Rusty and Velma Edwards have been active real estate investors for over six years. In that time, they have made many professional contacts. If one of their contacts—or a member of their "team"—helps the Edwards win a good deal, they make sure that the teammate also wins.

Last year, a Realtor teammate called Rusty about a deal. The Realtor had just found a foreclosure that had been originally listed for sale at $115,000 but, after 90 days on the market, had been reduced to $99,000. Rusty drove by immediately and inspected the house. It was nice, but he realized it would need a little cosmetic work, so Rusty and Velma didn't want to pay full price.

As soon as he returned to his office, Rusty called the Realtor back and made a $71,000 offer. The lender/seller declined this offer, but Rusty still thought his price was fair. Within 48 hours, he contacted the Realtor and made another offer at $71,500—just $500 more than his first rejected offer. The lender/seller accepted his second offer of $71,500.

Rusty was excited because he had made a great deal, but it was also a busy time for him. So he typed up some information about his deal, made copies, and took them to his next local real estate investors meeting. There, he placed the copies on the "deals" table for other investors to review. The next day, Rusty received a call and an offer from one of his fellow investors. Rusty sold, or flipped, the deal to another investor for $82,000. He made a good profit and passed on a handsome bonus to his Realtor.

40. GO WITH YOUR INSTINCTS

When it comes to trusting people, follow your gut feelings.
Doing so can pay huge rewards.

■ ■ ■

For good reason, investor Steve Slone always displays his "We Buy Houses" sign on his car. One day, a man who had seen Steve's sign approached him. He asked if Steve would like to buy his recently deceased brother's house. They agreed on a price and sealed the deal with a closing date 45 days later (because the house was in probate).

To be proactive, Steve decided to start renovations before he actually closed on the house, but he wanted some protection. At Steve's insistence, the seller signed several strongly worded documents guaranteeing that Steve would be paid for his improvements if, for any reason, their deal fell through. No documents are foolproof, though, so Steve still felt nervous but went with his gut feeling and trusted the seller and his motives. As a result of listening to his gut, Steve completed all the renovations, identified his own buyer, and sold the house for a $62,000 profit in a back-to-back closing.

41. A MESS FOR THE SELLER, A DEAL FOR YOU

You never really know which sellers will say yes
to your offer, nor why.

■ ■ ■

When Jeff Petracco first got into the business of buying and selling houses, someone told him that, if he wasn't feeling embarrassed that his offer was "ridiculous," then it was too high. As a result of that advice, Jeff offered a seller $100 a month for 80 months to buy what he thought was a $25,000 house. After the man accepted his offer, he discovered he was actually buying much more than the $25,000 house. In fact, Jeff was buying one parcel of land with five houses on it.

Jeff confesses to his naivety—he actually asked the seller if he was fully aware that he was selling all five houses. The man told him, "Yes, and thank goodness you are taking this mess off my hands!"

Jeff wasn't so sure about handling all the properties himself. So, soon after they sealed the deal, Jeff flipped the contract to another investor for a flat $7,500 fee. That investor then immediately flipped the contract to another investor (who kept the contract and the property) for a flat $8,000 fee, or a $500 profit. The paper trail can be confusing, but everyone seemed to walk away with a win-win feeling. The word from Jeff: "Needless to say, this business is fun!"

42. BUYING A DUPLEX 101

With a little information, effort, and belief, you can own a duplex
and pay less than what you currently pay in rent.

■ ■ ■

Because everyone understands the concept of paying rent, an opening question to new investors is, "How would you like to *collect* that rent as opposed to pay it?" Dan Auito, author of *Magic Bullets in Real Estate* (http://www.magicbullets.com), says that buying a duplex is a good way to get started.

"Duplexes are as easy to finance as a single-family home and, in many cases, allow you to qualify for a larger loan amount. That leads to using leverage and more of other people's money to get ahead faster," he says.

Say you find a duplex for $150,000 and your loan's interest rate is 6 percent. That totals $899.33 a month to pay principal and interest on a 30-year loan. Add to that insurance costs (use an average of $5 per $1,000 of home value), which is $750 ($5 × 150) a year for insurance, or $62.50 a month. Add to that annual taxes based on what the home is worth multiplied by a millage, or mill rate. Let's use a tax rate of $11 per $1,000 of the home's assessed value, which is $1,650.00 ($11 × 150) a year or $137.50 a month. Total the principal, interest, taxes, and insurance (collectively called PITI), and the monthly mortgage would be $1,099.33.

When you live in one side of the duplex and rent the other side for, say, $750 a month, you're left to pay $349.33 out of your own pocket. This amount is much lower than the rent you're likely paying now to live under someone else's roof and rules.

So how do you buy a duplex like this? By getting prequalified for a loan. Before applying for your loan, bring the following items to a bank's loan officer:

- Copies of three years of tax returns for first-time buyers, plus schedules and W-2 forms
- Copies of your most recent pay stubs from the last 30 days
- Copies of your most recent three months of bank statements
- A list of all creditors with names, addresses, and account numbers

With these documents, the loan officer can determine your assets and liabilities (net worth) as well as verify where you live, your credit history, and a host of other information that validates your ability to borrow money now and pay it back in the future.

Once your information has been reviewed and verified, the loan officer can preapprove you for a certain loan amount. That means you can begin your search for a home of your own. As a first-time homebuyer, you'll find programs that let you put as little as 3 to 5 percent down to buy a home and satisfy the lender's value guidelines. On a $150,000 loan, the down payment can range from $4,500 to $7,500.

With duplexes, the lender takes into account the fact that 75 percent of the rental income from the other side of the property can be used to offset your qualifying ratios. In this case, they can use 75 percent of the rental's $750 income to reduce the amount you must earn to qualify for what may appear to be an unaffordable loan. So 75 percent of $750 equals $562.50. Subtracting that amount from the original mortgage payment of $1,099.33 leaves a payment of $536.83, which the bank says you must qualify to repay every month. Can you see how, with a little information, effort, and belief, you can actually own something and pay less than what you are currently paying in rent?

What if you don't have money to get that loan and buy the duplex? Where can you get it? Savings, parents or grandparents, sale of valuable possessions, a second job, grants, gifts, trust funds, personal loans, cosigners—or combining these alternatives with a complementary loan program—usually gets the ball rolling. (Options and hard money-lenders come later as alternative funding and acquisition sources.) The bottom line is this: if you want something badly enough, there's always a way to finance it.

From the day you become the new owner, you've just created a passive income stream that gives you an extra $750 a month without your having to punch a clock or trade hours to earn money. Your new asset works for you day in and day out, generating income while you do other things. This is called leveraging your time and money in a beneficial way.

Notice that, at the closing of your purchase, the owners who sold you this property had to prorate or give you a share of the rents due and any security deposits tenants had given them. Add to that the likelihood that your first house payment won't come due until about a month and a half after you move in, and you find yourself with extra money—possibly for the first time ever if you're a brand-new investor.

Assuming you close on the 15th of the month, you'll have 45 days before your first payment comes due, you'll be credited with 15 days of rent, you'll receive all security deposits of the tenant and another month's rent on the first of the month from your tenant. You yourself will have no rent or house payment of your own to make for another whole month. Here's how that looks.

- Fifteen days of rent equal to $375
- A half month's rent as a security deposit equal to $375
- A full month's rent in another 15 days equal to $750
- No payment to the bank for another 30 days, and you're not paying rent any longer, so you get to keep that amount (let's say $500 a month)

■ Another payment to you for $750 from your tenant, as well as making your first mortgage payment of $1,099.33 on the first of the month 45 days later

If you decided to rent your second bedroom to a roommate, that person would pay $500 a month in rent and half your utilities as well. Thus, you'd be living in and owning this property for free.

Adding these up, you'd have $375 + $375 + $750 + $750 + $500 not being paid to your old landlord. You'll now have $2,750 as a result of your first month and a half of ownership. Subtract your mortgage payment of $1,099.33 and you're left with a reserve fund of $1,650.67.

Your next phase is to realize that you're now responsible for the welfare of another family or person because of your willingness to become a landlord. If you chose a good property by carefully examining plumbing, heating and A/C, electrical, foundation, structure, roof, location, and price, you should be well positioned to manage these duties successfully. You'll want to make improvements to the property, including painting, installing new carpet, repairs, and inexpensive landscaping. These add value to your property and keep your tenants happy, while not breaking the bank to cover the costs.

With $1,650.67 in your bank account, you're not Donald Trump just yet, but it's a start. Establish six-month reserve accounts and/or contingency funds, which will protect you in times of vacancies or when expensive unforeseen repair bills pop up (in addition to scheduled maintenance). Don't spend your reserves frivolously.

Let's look at your accomplishments. First, you've overcome fear and lack of understanding by acquiring your first property. In addition, you're offsetting expenses while saving money, establishing good credit while building assets, and gaining tax advantages while getting management, home buying, and repair education. Indeed, you can employ these skills for the rest of your life.

Let's assume it's two years after you purchased your first duplex. Taking into account that you bought a decent property in a good neighborhood and inflation and appreciation (as well as your improvements) have been adding value, your $150,000 duplex should command a new appraised value of $175,000. Here are the numbers.

- 3% annual inflation × $150,000 = $4,500 the first year.
- Add in appreciation of 5% × $150,000 equals $7,500.
- Add $150,000 + $7,500 + $4,500 = $162,000, which represents the property's new value for year one.

Do the same math on $162,000 for the second year, and you get $12,960 + $162,000 = $174,960 for year two.

During those two years, you've been paying a mortgage of $1,099.33 each month. The principal amount owed on your loan has been reduced by an additional $3,965.96, leaving you with a loan balance of $146,034.04. The difference between the newly appraised value of $175,000 and the current amount of $146,034.04 is $28,965.96. This number represents the equity, or value, that you currently own in the home.

Knowing this, it's possible to apply for and receive a home equity line of credit up to the full value of the new appraisal. Assuming that you haven't gone overboard buying vehicles and running up revolving debt, then the bank will likely approve this line of owner-occupied credit.

You can now use this line of credit to buy a $145,000 single-family home with a 20 percent down payment. A 20 percent deposit allows you to avoid paying private mortgage insurance (known as PMI), thereby creating an affordable new mortgage on this new residence.

Let's not forget that, as the value of your duplex has risen, the rents should also increase along the same lines. Instead of $750, you'd reasonably expect to get $800 per month, per side, sending $1,600 a month to your bank account. Unfortunately, you still have to pay for 28 more years on the original loan amount, so you will make that good old $1,099.33 payment as usual. That leaves you with $500.67 a month left over to pay that new equity line back with. Your new $29,000 equity line, which you used as a down payment on your new home, costs you $336.71 at 7 percent for 10 years. Now, $500.36 –

$336.71 leaves you with $163.96 left to maintain a reserve account for vacancies and maintenance/repairs.

What have you just accomplished? Steps toward a secure lifestyle while using your asset base to buy more investment property.

43. MODULAR HOMES CAN BE VIABLE INVESTMENTS

Modular homes may offer investors the best way yet
to achieve no-money-down rewards.

■ ■ ■

Over the last 30 years, Stephen Starbuck has invested in real estate with a keen eye for lease-options. He has also been a mortgage broker with a skill for helping others—especially those with poor credit histories—buy their own homes. Over the last few years, many high-dollar communities have grown up on the old Southern cotton plantations near Lake Oconee, 45 minutes southeast of Atlanta. There, lakeside land prices range from $400,000 to $1,000,000 per lot, but land still gets sold quickly. The Ritz-Carlton luxury hotel chain recently built a hotel with 251 rooms and an 81-hole golf course on 8,000 acres.

In the whirlwind of so much high-dollar building, local newspapers (and Starbuck) noted that few affordable homes were available for all the service-industry personnel moving into the locale. He had already researched, developed, and leased out two modular homes in north Georgia, then decided to move south and build homes for the newest "worker bee" community.

Starbuck already knew the lenders he wanted to work with. They were willing to make construction loans based on the appraised value of the finished house. If he were an occupant of the home, the lenders would lend him up to 85 percent of its appraised value; as a nonoccupant investor, he could borrow between 75 and 80 percent of appraised value. His normal construction costs would be between 65 and 70 percent of appraised value, and the 5 to 15 percent spread between his loan and his cost would serve as his contractor's salary while he "constructed" the houses. As a bonus, Starbuck also knew the modular home manufacturer that he would deal with. He'd met many manufacturers at home shows and tradeshows and had found a favorite few that offer high-quality, comprehensive service.

Usually, Starbuck's biggest problem is finding land. Even though most modular houses meet or exceed the quality of standard, stick-built houses, some subdivision covenants prohibit their development. Once he finds the land, he develops a budget based on his house, land, and contractor cost. He also develops his draw schedule, which is a timeline showing when he will need his lender to give him money. All construction loans make partial payments according to a timeline. Most construction loans pay out in up to 12 installments, but Starbuck only needs 3. His lenders really appreciate that simplicity.

Before long, Starbuck incurred his only real out-of-pocket expense—hiring an appraiser to give a "subject to" appraisal for the house on the land. Then, armed with his budget, his draw schedule, and his appraisal, Starbuck applied for and received his loan. He felt proud that he could develop his first homes in three months and re-sell or lease (usually with an option to buy) a high-quality, brand-new house with 20 percent equity built-in.

Shortly after completing it, Starbuck leased one of his Lake Oconee modular homes to a woman with a poor credit history. For a $2,500 nonrefundable fee, he also gave her an option to purchase the house at its current price within the first three months of the lease or at an independently appraised value within two years.

A few months later, he became concerned when she sent him a bad rent check written on a closed business account. He called her. She said that she had been on business trips and had asked a friend to write the check for her. Apparently her friend had used the wrong checkbook, which is why the check bounced. She immediately made good on her rent.

Starbuck proudly says that, since she first leased the house, this tenant has already paid off a state tax lien and cleaned up her credit cards. With very little risk on the deal, clearly everyone has come out a winner.

44. LOCATION, LOCATION, LOCATION

Schools and city services directly affect property values, so buy investment properties in desirable, well-serviced areas.

■ ■ ■

The Fletchers purchased a brick, two-family house in 1968 for about $22,000 in a nice neighborhood on the east side of Detroit. Says Matt, "I can remember my father saying the rent money from the upper flat covered the house payment each month. My family lived there for about 25 years."

In the 1980s, Matt's neighborhood began to deteriorate, and it became difficult for the family to attract a good renter for the upper flat. Having learned valuable lessons from owning other properties, the family decided to move. Their home sold for $39,900—not much appreciation on a 25-year investment. In 1968, the same type of home in the nearby suburb of Grosse Pointe could have been purchased for exactly the same price. Over the years, though, houses in Grosse Pointe appreciated very quickly, while houses in Detroit appreciated very little. Property even went down in many areas. Had Matt's family purchased a home in Grosse Pointe, 25 years later it would have sold it for well over $100,000 instead of $39,900.

Here's why. The good reputation of Grosse Pointe got even better over the years. While the school system in Detroit deteriorated during that time, in Grosse Pointe, it just kept getting better. Today, that community has one of the best-rated public school systems in the country, while Detroit public schools are among the worst. The reason? Money. It's always the money. People with money moved to suburbs like Grosse Pointe; people without good jobs and good incomes were left behind. This activity directly affects property values.

Says Matt, now a home inspector (http://www.miproperty.com), "The neighborhood surrounding our old Detroit home continues to deteriorate. The house my father sold for $39,900 in the early 1990s is probably worth less now. But I'm not beating up on the city of Detroit. Recently, the city and its services have begun to turn around, and property values are beginning to move up. I would consider buying property in certain areas of Detroit today. I predict the city will continue to rebound."

45. THE "REAL DEAL" AT AUCTIONS

Never pay more than *you* think a property is worth at auctions.

■ ■ ■

When Matt Fletcher and his father walked into an auction to bid on houses for sale, they had to show a cashier's check of $2,000 just to be admitted. Matt recalls, "One of the men holding the auction struck up a conversation and asked how we planned to pay for the property we were bidding on. My dad asked if they took cashier's checks. 'Absolutely,' the man replied, and took our name, phone number, and address of the property we were interested in. Later, we found out why."

They had come to the auction looking for a deal, but their hopes were soon dashed when people started bidding out of control. They bid more than the properties were worth and more than they could afford to pay. "We just looked at each other with our mouths hanging open each time a property was overbid. When the one we wanted came up for bid, the same thing happened. We estimated it was worth $12,000. When it sold for $22,000, we got up and left.

"Three days later, a man from the auction company called because the winning bidder didn't come up with enough money. He asked if we were still interested in that property and what would we be willing to pay. We said $12,000 seemed fair, he accepted, and we closed the next day."

The Fletchers rented out the house for a couple of years for $400 a month, then sold it for $30,000 on a conventional loan, making $25,000 overall. Matt's experience shows that, at auctions, the competitiveness of human nature can cause people to bid and pay more than they normally would.

46. CREATIVE MORTGAGE SURGERY

Even when mortgage complications put up roadblocks, you can often find a way to get through the red tape.

■ ■ ■

A medical doctor and investor in Houston wanted to liquidate his inventory of approximately 99 rental houses. One of the houses that investor Judy Cook was looking to buy had more mortgages than it was worth: a first mortgage, a second mortgage, and a third mortgage. It may have had a lien or two as well.

Because of the mortgage situation, Judy showed the doctor that she really couldn't purchase the property. This house needed a lot of work. It had been abused by the last four tenants, and the owner had not replaced anything. The roof was starting to fall in, and the garage doors already had. They even found cat hairs sticking up out of the floor in the living room from a dead cat that had rotted in the cement. When Judy told the doctor about the mortgage dilemma he was in, he came up with a plan of his own. First, he had to find out who owned the first mortgage.

This happened when banks and mortgage companies were in disarray in the state of Texas. Few people knew where mortgages were, because they had been sold so many times. Many banks had their assets turned over to the Resolution Trust Company; then other companies had bought mortgage loans from the Resolution Trust, while the FDIC also had control of certain things. In addition, Texas bankers had lent a lot of money to borrowers in Mexico who had subsequently defaulted. The price of real estate in some of the cities was going upside down because of the interest rates. All this caused problems for the lenders at the time.

The doctor's plan was to purchase the first lien on the property. He couldn't purchase it in his own name because he was the payor. Instead, he set it up in the name of his stepson, who had a different last name, so no one would know the two men were related.

Now that the stepson owned the first lien that had not been paid on for a long time, the timing was perfect to foreclose on the house as soon as possible. Judy reminded them that Texas was one of the fastest foreclosure states, and now was their best chance to get out of the property.

So Judy showed up at the foreclosure sale. That day, a total of 900 people showed up. Chaos prevailed; there was no order, no one with a gavel, just people stating that they were the trustees (or the substitute trustees) on given real estate notes. The officials announced the next foreclosing auction, someone read the legal description and the physical address, and then asked for bids on that property.

Because Judy was familiar with the house itself and had predetermined the amount to bid, she put in her offer. Judy continues the story by saying, "Then came two men who knew that I bid at foreclosure sales and usually bought good deals. They proceeded to bid up my offer.

"Not liking this at all, I had to do some quick thinking, so I asked them if they knew about the dead cat in the living room. Of course, there really was a dead cat in the living room. I knew it, but they hadn't checked out this house. They were only going on what I was bidding, thinking a little bit more from them would still make it a good deal.

"But when I pointed out that they hadn't visited the property at all—and told them this deal really was too risky—they backed off, and I bought it at a very low price.

"It turned out to be a good house for me," Judy says. "I bought it, rented it, then sold it for a handsome profit."

47. STAY OPEN TO NEW BUYING POSSIBILITIES

Being friendly and open to new situations can lead to lucky meetings and lucrative deals.

■ ■ ■

Sergeant First Class Kristopher Bender turned down two senior promotions so that he could leave the army. While in the army, he had taken one young fellow who lacked discipline under his wing. He'd shown him the ropes, encouraged him to be a responsible soldier, and made a fast friend for himself. In doing so, he really impressed the young fellow's father, a successful businessman and real estate investor. That father, in turn, took Kris under his wing and gave him business and investment advice. Before long, Kris believed that he, too, could be a successful businessman and investor.

Kris and his wife, Michelle, talked about their goals and started playing CASHFLOW 101, the board game invented by Robert Kiyosaki, author of *Rich Dad, Poor Dad.* Their mindset changed and they eagerly awaited the day when they could start investing. When Michelle started making enough money to cover all their bills with her salary only, she urged Kris to go for it and start investing in real estate. "It was now or never," she said.

The Benders live near Clarksville, Tennessee, close to the Fort Campbell military base. Kris expected that his first investment property would be housing for military personnel, but it didn't happen that way. One day, the Benders went to check out a Toyota that they were interested in buying. They discovered that the older lady who owned the Toyota also owned some investment properties. She liked Kris, and when he told her that he wanted to buy some investment property, she told him that she was selling some. She was getting divorced and wanted to make a clean break, so she was liquidating her assets.

In April 2003, the Benders bought their first investment property—a commercial office building in Melbur, Kentucky—from the Toyota lady. It seemed like a perfect investment. It was a triple net, that is the tenant agreed to pay all applicable property taxes, insurance, repairs, utilities, and maintenance. And their first and only tenant in that building with a lease until 2008 was a stable one—the United States Postal Service.

Now they say that looking for a car led to their first big investment—all because they were personable with the seller and open to new possibilities.

48. YOU DON'T ALWAYS GET WHAT YOU ASK FOR

Carefully decide what's okay with you when you ask
for compromises on a deal.

■ ■ ■

As a Realtor, Mercedes Rezvanpour continually sticks up for her clients who invest in real estate. Recently, she helped an investor client buy a house in East Point, a heavily invested area of Atlanta. The house has three bedrooms, two-and-one-half bathrooms, and a full-daylight basement; that is, one with windows allowing daylight to shine inside. The lender for this house had foreclosed on the original owner's loan and taken possession of it, then paid to have the house completely rehabbed before selling it. Mercedes's client offered

$125,000, and that offer was accepted. Before closing, her client received an appraisal valuing the house at between $150,000 and $160,000.

In the purchase and sales agreement, Mercedes had added a stipulation requiring that the lender give her client a satisfactory termite letter at closing. A termite letter comes from a company that has inspected and treated the property for termites and says that the property is free of termites. But at the closing meeting, Mercedes immediately noticed two things. First, the lender was not giving her client a termite letter, and, second, she was only receiving a 2.5 percent commission rather than her usual 3 percent commission. Mercedes discussed these facts with her client and then asked the lender's representative what they were going to do about it. The lender's representative said that the lender would not give her client a termite letter and that the commission would not change. He knew that similar houses received between five and ten offers a day from investors; if her client didn't want to buy this house "as is," another investor certainly would. So Mercedes decided she would be okay with this if her client was. He agreed, and the compromise still brought her a tidy commission.

49. KEEP THE DOOR OPEN WHEN OPPORTUNITY KNOCKS

Listen and consider offers carefully, because good opportunities can keep knocking on your door.

■ ■ ■

In 1998, Fred and Sandra Clark (pseudonyms) bought a 2,400-square-foot duplex in Nashville's upscale Belmont Hillsboro neighborhood for $145,000. It was an ideal rental property located just south of Music Row, between the Vanderbilt and Belmont University grounds. They bought the property from their real estate agent's brother, an investor who had carefully maintained it but had not completely improved it. Consequently, they added central heat and air conditioning to both units, replumbed the duplex, and gave it a general facelift. Tenants stayed for long periods of time, referrals came quickly, and vacancies were short-lived. The average monthly rents they received were $1,750.

In 2003, a husband and wife living across the street asked the Clarks if they'd be interested in selling the duplex. This couple had become successful singers and songwriters who needed additional space to accommodate an in-house professional recording studio as well as room for relatives who would be visiting from Texas.

Although they hadn't previously thought about selling the property, they talked it over and decided not to sell it at that time. They just didn't want to lose their excellent return on investment. A few months after their initial request, the couple asked again. Fred and Sandra reconsidered but declined again.

Several months later, their son moved to Nashville, and, while helping Fred work on the property one day, he had a chance to meet the couple who wanted to purchase the duplex. The two men both loved photography and hit it off famously. Later, the couple asked Fred and Sandra *again* if they were interested in selling the property. This time, the Clarks listened to the advice of their eldest son—a real estate attorney—and seriously considered the offer. The more they considered it, the better they liked it.

Like dedicated investors, they started negotiating a sales price. Over the next few months, the musical couple were traveling and performing on tour while negotiating terms and preparing for closing from the road. Just before year's end, they closed the sale on the property with the Clarks at a selling price of $292,000.

The Clarks had only owned the property for six years, but during those six years, Nashville real estate values soared. Shortly before closing, an appraiser valued the property at $286,000. Because the Clarks weren't eager to sell, they asked the couple to pay a small premium. So the couple paid $6,000 over the appraised value.

Happily, everyone walked away from this deal feeling good about it.

50. LUCK CAN WORK ON YOUR SIDE

Sometimes you can just be in the right place at the right time.

■ ■ ■

Like many successful investors, Rusty Edwards was a general contractor before he discovered real estate investing—or it discovered him.

Several years ago, Rusty and his wife Velma decided to build their own house. They found the perfect property and listed their current house for sale. They planned on selling it and living with Rusty's mother for the five or six months that it would take to build their new house.

One day, when one of their cars started acting up, Rusty took it in to his local mechanic's shop for an inspection. While waiting in the shop, he overheard an interesting conversation. A young woman who was related to the shop owners came inside and asked if they might be interested in buying a house and three acres that she'd inherited from her aunt. The shop owners said that they weren't interested, but Rusty spoke up and said that he might be interested. The woman told him where it was, and, later that day, the Edwards drove out there to look it over.

They liked the property, so they offered the young woman $21,000 for the house and the three acres. Apparently, when she had inherited the property, it was under lease to some difficult tenants. She had gotten rid of them and declared she'd had her fill of being a landlord. As a result of that experience, she eagerly accepted their offer and even agreed to take back a second mortgage for $7,000. Later, Rusty learned that the woman was trying to sell the second mortgage for cash, so he bought his mortgage back for 50 cents on the dollar—the best rate that she had found.

The Edwards quickly closed on the property and started rehabbing it. Although they were fixing up the house for themselves, they only planned to live in it until they finished building their house elsewhere. It wasn't ideal for them. Specifically, the septic system was in disrepair and the land, which bordered on the road, was zoned for commercial development.

While they were working one day, Rusty found $40 underneath a discarded rug—a sweet piece of luck. But on another day, when he was working alone, he got especially lucky. A real estate agent drove up to the house and asked if the house and land were for sale. As many investors would say, Rusty told him, "Of course. Just about anything I've got is for sale." The agent told Rusty that he knew someone who would probably like to buy it. Rusty asked, "Are you serious about this? Because I don't have time to fool around—I have work to do." The agent said he was 100 percent serious and that he could immediately write an earnest money check on behalf of his buyer. Rusty called Velma and they decided that the offer was reasonable. He stopped working on the house immediately, and they sold this property for a $10,000 profit.

This was a lucky deal from start to finish for Rusty and Velma.

51. WIN-WIN FOR CAT LADY AND INVESTORS

You can never predict who your buyer might be.

■ ■ ■

Several years ago, Ginny Pitts and one of her investment partners in Nashville, Tennessee, investigated buying a group of five occupied, single-family houses from an investor. Before making the purchase, they decided to inspect each of the houses personally.

When they arrived at the last of the five houses, they were bowled over by a foul smell reeking through the front door. Through a window beside the front door, they could see tall, dark stacks of unknown materials. Because her partner was wearing a business suit and heels, Ginny decided to inspect this house alone.

Once inside, she unearthed a small pathway between stacks of clothes, newspapers, tattered furniture, and unidentifiable items in the living room. She watched cats eating from bowls atop these stacks piled everywhere. That's when the tenant proudly told her, "I have 14 cats!"

As she looked around the room more closely, Ginny noticed running roaches, buzzing flies, rotting food containers, and a few new yet equally foul smells. She was mentally calculating rehab costs when the tenant opened the first bedroom door for her inspection. She cheerfully pointed out that there really was a bed under the piles, and this bedroom even had two closets, a "his" and a "hers." Ginny couldn't see them; all she could do was be polite and say, "How nice."

Then Ginny backed out into the hallway and tried to push open the door to the second bedroom. Cobwebs littered the face of the door; something on the other side kept her from opening it more than a few inches. "Oh, there's nothing in there. That's my junk room," the tenant told her.

When Ginny returned to her office, she recounted in colorful detail what she saw in this home of 14 cats, and thus began the legend of the Cat Lady.

A short time later, Ginny and her investment partner decided to purchase all five houses including the Cat Lady's house (even though they dreaded dealing with its rehab). Soon after the purchase, they sent all the tenants notice that they had 30 days to vacate, because the new owners were going to renovate and then sell each house. Within a few days of sending the letter, the Cat Lady called their office. Ginny actually expected to see tears from her and answer questions like "Who'll take me with all my cats?"

Instead, the Cat Lady asked, "How much will you be selling the house for, anyway?"

"After renovations, the house would sell for $69,900," Ginny replied.

"How much will it take to fix it up?"

"It would take around $15,000."

"What will you sell it to *me* for?" the Cat Lady asked.

Ginny made some calculations and then named a price that was about $7,000 more than she had paid for it. Within a few weeks, the Cat Lady received approval for a conventional loan plus $15,000 for rehab costs.

Ginny was especially pleased they'd sold the house without going through the grueling process of rehabbing it. And, at the closing, The Cat Lady told them she was planning a yard sale very soon.

52. LOW BID CAN FORFEIT QUICK SALE

When a seller names a reasonable price, don't get too greedy.
Closing the deal quickly can often be more beneficial than
holding out for a lower price.

■ ■ ■

Investor Barbara Downing had located two beautiful, one-acre building lots in a lake neighborhood near Atlanta. The lots were originally listed for sale at $17,000 each. After time passed and no buyers stepped forward, the owner dropped the listing price to $12,000 each. At that point, a prospective buyer offered the seller $10,000 per lot, but Barbara had already offered the seller the full list price of $12,000 per lot. Not surprisingly, the seller accepted Barbara's offer.

Within 30 minutes of coming to an agreement with the seller, Barbara received a call from the same prospective buyer who had offered $10,000 for each lot. Apparently he was quite desperate to own them. He offered her $18,000 each, which she immediately accepted. At the back-to-back closing that followed, she pocketed $12,000 for her efforts. "If I had been greedy and didn't go with the seller's price, I would have missed out on this opportunity," she says.

53. GETTING FACTS LANDS YOUNG INVESTOR A HOME

Dig deep into county records and look for properties that
can turn into good deals.

■ ■ ■

For his 18th birthday and graduation present, Judy Cook's son, Ulrick, asked to take the real estate investment program that his mom taught. Ulrick said he wanted to buy a house near his grandma's place, because he could count on her providing lunch during the weeks he'd be rehabbing his house. About the same time, he spotted a run-down house on Sunwick Street. With its tall grass and broken windows, it looked as though no one lived there. He declared to his mom, "That's it. That's the one I'm gonna buy."

Judy, being the mentor and coach she was, told Ulrick that the buying process involved finding three or four houses first, then negotiating his best deal on one of them. But he responded by stating, "Why? I've already found the house I want; that's the one." That's when Judy decided to back off and let him do the rest of the work on his own.

The next day, Ulrick went to the courthouse to locate the name of the owner of this house on Sunwick Street. He quickly found the owner's name. When Judy challenged him with, "But now you have to *find* the owner," which can often take a long time, he answered that he already had. Judy told him, "Next, you have to go talk about price and terms with the owner."

The following day, Judy went with her son to see the owner, a broker. She thought, "Now I know why he was so easy to find; he is a Houston real estate broker with a big office. So much for getting a low price." But she let Ulrick do the talking and the broker told him, "Son, I'd love to sell you that house, but I don't own it."

As the pair walked away to go out to the car, Judy asked, "How is it you didn't know who owns the house?" Ulrick replied with confidence, "I *do* know who owns it. That broker."

So they turned around and went back in. Judy asked for an explanation on the ownership issue, and the broker said that seven years before, he had filed bankruptcy and given all his rental houses over to the bankruptcy trustee. Now the *courts* owned the house.

Because of his research, Ulrick had known this, but he also knew that the deed still carried the broker's name. After seven years, the bankruptcy was over. This house, which had been overlooked by everyone, was now actually back in the hands of the broker. So, finally, the broker realized what was going on and accepted Ulrick's money as the buyer. Ulrick had already prepared a deed and got the broker to sign it.

Before long, Ulrick got his photo in the *Houston Chronicle* for all the renovation work he'd done on this three-bedroom, one-bath home. The article in the paper praised this young man for taking on this project to fix an old, abandoned house in an otherwise nice neighborhood.

54.   ALWAYS TIME
TO RECONSIDER

Always maintain the courage to walk away from a deal. It's like
the bus—even if you miss it, another one will always come along.

■ ■ ■

Investor David Finkel (http://www.resultsnow.com) advises,
"Looking back at all the properties I have bought, flipped, and lease-
optioned, the one common denominator for all the borderline deals
is that, at some point in the negotiation, I had crossed over to the
point where I felt I had to do the deal.

"But, if ever you hear yourself saying these words—even if it's
to yourself—push back your chair, get up from the negotiating table,
and walk away. I'm serious about this. If the deal is that good, a
small break while you take a moment by yourself won't stop the
deal. And by taking this time, you might just keep your ego and
your emotions from pushing you to make a deal that means lots of
work and risk for little real profit."

55.   A LUCKY
ABANDONMENT

Some blessings come in strange disguises. Be open to them.

■ ■ ■

Investor Susan Benting had originally designated a property in
New Mexico to exchange in compliance with IRS Code Section
1031, tax deferral exchange of similar properties. But for several
reasons, she later decided to designate a Tennessee property as her
exchange property instead.

Around that time, one of her friends fell on hard times. His wife left him with a two-year-old daughter, a new business, and no way to close on his mobile home and land contract. Susan decided to use her money and 1031-Exchange to help him. She bought his home and land contract, then leased the mobile home back to him.

For three months everything went well, but then he missed payments for two months and abandoned the mobile home. After he left, Susan had the mobile home inspected and discovered that the furnace was drawing carbon monoxide into it. Her friend and his daughter could have died from carbon monoxide poisoning or a furnace explosion if they had not moved out. This simple act of abandonment saved the day for everyone.

56. THE DAY IT PAID
TO GET BORED

Keeping your mind open to new opportunities can pay off.

■ ■ ■

While at a meeting that Judy Cook had to attend regarding her Montana real estate license, she got really bored. At a break, she went out to buy a newspaper and was able to keep in good spirits by reading it in class.

As she perused the classifieds, she spotted an ad about an apartment building for sale in her hometown of Ronan. She says, "I called the owner, and he said we could meet at a local restaurant the next day. So we met, then walked down the street to the building. (My hometown is really small.) Joe showed me several of the eight units and the basement. He had three or four rented, and a couple of the tenants weren't paying rent at the time."

Judy had done her homework and knew that if all eight units housed good tenants and every tenant paid the going price each month, the complex could bring in $2,800 a month before expenses. The ad had stated that Joe wanted $140,000, and, Judy notes, "When buying rental property, that wouldn't be a bad deal."

However, she had already talked to some people in town who said it couldn't be a good deal because Joe was a leading businessman in town, and if he couldn't make it work, then no one could.

"But I didn't listen. I sat down with Joe back at that same coffee spot. He told me that he'd done some checking around and knew who I was, too. He said that there was no use trying to get the price down because he wasn't going to go below $130,000, and that he would have to charge me 10 percent on that money." Even with those conditions, Judy closed the deal and got the keys to the place that day.

She made small improvements immediately. To make the dark entryway more attractive, she changed the lights in the hallway and replaced the old ugly carpet with sand-colored press-and-stick tile. Then she painted the entrance doors. "All in all, I didn't spend very much money. My deposits from rent were equal to my repair bills to make this place look really nice."

With this new ownership, all the old tenants except one moved out. "The one who stayed asked if, because I was doubling the rent, he could make that payment in two parts—one on the 1st and one on the 15th," says Judy.

This building has now been 100 percent occupied for more than 6 months, and after all its expenses are paid, it nets $1,000 a month. "It really paid me to get bored that day!" Judy concludes.

57. FINDING DEALS CLOSE TO HOME

Sometimes you can find excellent deals in your own backyard.

■ ■ ■

Tom and Jennifer Hamilton first purchased a rental house in their neighborhood, just a few blocks from their own home in Nashville, Tennessee. Because Tom enjoys being a handyman, he has always taken good care of his properties. Because he's a new investor, he's kept a close eye on changes in his neighborhood.

Several years ago, while working on his rental house, he noticed that the house next door—nearly identical to his own rental—was for sale. He told Jennifer about it, and they decided to check it out. They contacted the listing real estate agent and arranged to have the house shown to them formally. After the showing, they agreed that it was in good condition, equal to their rental, so they made an offer to buy it. They chose not to tell the agent or the owner that they owned and rented out the house next door; they didn't want to give the owner or listing agent any reason to up the ante. Their offer was quickly accepted.

Tom and Jennifer already owned their home and one rental, so they had positive cash flow and didn't have to use credit cards to buy this new rental property. They did, however, have to list all of their assets on their loan application.

When they closed on their second rental house, the listing real estate agent sat next to the closing attorney and, during that time, noticed on one of the closing documents that the Hamiltons already owned the house next door to the one they were buying. The listing agent was surprised and told them so, but she didn't rock the boat. Everyone walked away happy: the seller had cash, the listing agent had cash, and the Hamiltons had two rental houses next door to each other. To them, that meant good rentals close by, neither needing much maintenance, and both in a good, up-and-coming neighborhood.

The Hamiltons kept both rental houses for several years, until Jennifer's parents made them an offer they couldn't refuse. Her parents owned a small vacation house nestled in a remote but highly prized, wooded area of Maine. Her parents wanted to keep using the house, but they also wanted to cash out some of their equity in it. They offered to sell the vacation house to Jennifer and Tom for a reasonable price as long as they could still use it periodically.

Jennifer and Tom discussed the fact that they were both from "up North," she from Maine and he from New Jersey, and that they really enjoyed visiting the vacation house themselves. It didn't hurt that this lovely house was skyrocketing in value, too. They agreed to purchase it from her parents, although when they reviewed their finances, they discovered they'd have to sell one of their rental houses to afford it. Considering market appreciation and the effects of capital gains taxes, they decided to sell their second rental house in Nashville to pay for the vacation house in Maine.

Twice, the Hamiltons found good deals close to home—in their Nashville neighborhood and in their family's vacationland. They are confident that they made the right investment choice with all of these properties.

■ TIPS

33. Keep your eyes open for For Sale by Owner signs that can't be seen easily.

34. Research local real estate regulations and know property values in the area you want to invest in.

35. You can reap dozens of personal and professional rewards by attending a National Real Estate Investors Association (NREIA) cruise.

36. It's never about the property; it's always about the motivation of the seller.

37. If you know the full history of a property, you can enhance both your confidence and your position during a buying transaction.

38. Sometimes you can get a fantastic buy simply by honestly helping someone who is having tough times.

39. Build a networking team and show appreciation when team members come through for you.

40. When it comes to trusting people, follow your gut feelings. Doing that can pay huge rewards.

41. You never really know which sellers will say "yes" to your offer, nor why.

42. With a little information, effort, and belief, you can own a duplex and pay less than what you currently pay in rent.

43. Modular homes may offer investors the best way yet to achieve no-money-down rewards.

44. Schools and city services directly affect property values, so buy investment properties in desirable, well-serviced areas.

45. Never pay more than you think a property is worth at auctions!

46. Even when mortgage complications put up roadblocks, you can always find a way to get through the red tape.

47. Being friendly and open to new situations can lead to lucky meetings and lucrative deals.

48. Carefully decide what's "okay" with you when you ask for compromises on a deal.

49. Listen and consider offers carefully because good opportunities can keep knocking on your door.

50. Sometimes you can just be in the right place at the right time.

51. You can never predict who your buyer might be.

52. When a seller names a reasonable price, don't get too greedy. Closing the deal quickly can often be more beneficial than holding out for a lower price.

53. Dig deep into county records and look for properties that can turn into good deals.

54. Always maintain the courage to walk away from a deal. It's like the bus—even if you miss it, another one will always come along.

55. Some blessings come in strange disguises. Be open to them.

56. Keeping your mind open to new opportunities can pay off.

57. Sometimes you can find excellent deals in your own backyard.

PART 3

FINANCIAL IDEAS

■ ■ ■

You found a great piece of real estate. You checked comparable sales prices, and you have a fair purchase price in mind. You don't have enough cash to buy that property right now, so you think about trying to find an investment partner. This is your first deal, though, and you want to do it on your own, so you decide to forget about acquiring partners for now.

Your first approach is to see if the seller will offer you favorable terms or sell you the property in exchange for a mortgage from you. Sometimes, you can get very favorable terms with seller financing. If you don't have time to get a loan or the bank won't give you one, you might be able to swing a deal using your credit card. It's been done.

If you do have time to get a loan and you think that the bank will give you one, you need to find a lender. Most successful real estate investors can quickly and easily obtain great financing from any number of lenders. Some real estate investors buy their investments through special arrangements like 1031-Exchanges, assumable loans, wraparound mortgages, and various forms of seller financing. Those real estate investors become successful when they look for deals that match very specific criteria.

Many investors buy most of their investments with ordinary loans from commercial or private lenders. If you're buying land and operating a business, then you might be able to qualify for a Small

Business Administration (SBA) loan or other forms of government-sponsored business loans. Just be careful to do your homework, because those loans come with special requirements.

Commercial and private lenders usually ease their rather rigid rules when lending to organized and experienced real estate investors. If you want to maximize your success as a real estate investor, be sure to learn about special arrangements. At the same time, make sure that you always appear organized and experienced to lenders. Impress those lenders, and they'll be impressed by you—for your first transaction and for every one that follows.

The stories that follow share some creative solutions that investors have found to work through their financing challenges.

58. TURN TO CREDIT CARD ADVANCES IN A PINCH

Use credit card financing judiciously. It can save
the day—and your deal.

■ ■ ■

Like many successful investors, Tom Hamilton occasionally listens to talk radio while driving his car. Back in the mid-1980s, Tom was driving around and heard an interview with Robert G. Allen, author of the ever-popular real estate tome, *Nothing Down*. During previous radio broadcasts, he had heard about the benefits of real estate investing, but something about Allen's interview really lit a fire for him. He didn't have friends or family who were investors but still decided that real estate investing might be just the thing for him. So, every time he drove around town, he started keeping his eyes open for real estate deals—anywhere and everywhere.

One day, in his own neighborhood, he drove down a small, block-long street that he'd never really seen before. That's how he found his first rental house.

The same evening he'd spotted the house, Tom and his wife, Jennifer, stopped by and looked it over. It was a small starter house in a new, up-and-coming neighborhood. The house itself measured right at 800 square feet and had two bedrooms and one bath, all for a decent price.

Like most first-time investors, Tom and Jennifer felt nervous about taking this financial plunge, but they thought it over and decided it was a good deal. So good, in fact, that they'd take out a second mortgage on their own house to pay for it.

At about the same time they submitted a successful offer to buy the new house, they filed documents asking for a second mortgage on their home. Their timing looked good. They would close their second mortgage and, within a week or so, they could use proceeds from the second mortgage to close on their first rental investment property.

As seasoned real estate professionals know, closings seldom occur on time, and Tom and Jennifer's second mortgage transaction was no exception. Two weeks before they were scheduled to close on their purchase, their lender postponed the second mortgage and scheduled it to close one week after the closing on the intended rental property. At first, Tom and Jennifer didn't know what to do. Then they realized that, if they took cash advances on all their credit cards, they'd have just enough cash to cover their down payment on the house. With little hesitation, they maxed out their credit cards with cash advances at 21 percent interest and closed on the rental house. Then, one week later, they closed the second mortgage on their home and were able to use those funds to pay off their credit cards completely.

Tom and Jennifer successfully used cash advances on their credit cards to buy their first rental house. Because they were able to pay off their credit cards completely and immediately, they avoided the extra costs that usually arise when credit card companies apply payments first toward purchases and last toward the higher-rate cash advances. As it turns out, they made an excellent purchase and, to this day, the Hamiltons still own that little house.

59. CREATE RESERVE ACCOUNTS

No one keeps extra money around to cover repairs
and emergencies, so put some of your rental income
into a reserve account.

■ ■ ■

John Franklin (a pseudonym) is a firm believer that, "No one ever has any extra money," and that if you don't put some aside for repairs and problems, you'll spend it.

Like clockwork, John sets aside some of his rental income by putting it into a reserve account for future needs. He says, "If you save 10 percent of what you make every month, you will retire well-off. If you save 20 percent, you won't ever have any financial problems. If you save 25 percent, you will be very, very wealthy. If you live at a standard that's about five years behind what your income would allow you to live on, then you will be a very wealthy individual."

Most people don't plan to fail; most people fail to plan. As the author of *The Millionaire Next Door* has pointed out in his book, most young people tend to live on next to nothing. But when they graduate from college, they often go out and buy things: new cars, furniture, TVs, and lots more. But the people who live below their means are the ones likely to become wealthy.

John plans for the future by putting money aside in his rental escrow accounts, calculating the amount based on the law of averages. A new roof typically lasts 30 years, for example, so each year he puts into escrow 1/30th of the amount that he expects to spend on a replacement roof. A new water heater typically lasts 12 years, so each year John puts into escrow 1/12th of the amount that he expects to spend on a replacement water heater. He can't always perfectly estimate the life of everything in his rentals, but his escrow practice has kept him solvent when "unexpected" costs did arise over the years.

60. UNDERSTAND SBA REGULATIONS FROM THE START

Make sure you understand what government agencies like the
Small Business Administration require before starting to build
your dream property.

■ ■ ■

Larry Elliott had often dreamt about developing and operating
his own hunting and fishing camp and marina. He was able to use
construction loan proceeds from a bank to start developing the land
near Saginaw Bay. Around the time the building was 80 percent
complete, the lending bank's president told him that the Small Business Administration (SBA) was ready to talk about giving him a permanent loan.

Together, Larry and the bank president met with the SBA representative. As they made their presentation to request an SBA loan,
they showed their completed documents and photos of the development. After they'd finished their full pitch, their SBA contact said
the camp and marina looked like a wonderful development, but because it was well underway, the SBA couldn't fund it. If only Larry
had come to him before he started developing, he was told, then he'd
probably have had no problem getting SBA funding. Ah, the value
of hindsight!

61. QUICK RESPONSES, READY FUNDS

Develop your borrowing power so you can move quickly
on big deals that come your way.

■ ■ ■

Every successful investor advises new investors to return calls as soon as possible so they don't miss any deals. But there's much more to investing than that. If you don't want to miss good deals, you also need to build and maintain your credit and your track record. After decades of experience in the real estate business, John Anderson (a pseudonym) understands the value of maintaining his borrowing power.

Not long ago, an established Nashville, Tennessee, investor decided to liquidate his real estate portfolio. Early one morning, he asked John and several other investors to make him offers. John called the investor back within two hours, but the others didn't call him for days. John was able to deliver $860,000 cash to take over 25 of the investor's properties and close within 30 days—and he had the credit available to borrow much more. While his colleagues procrastinated, John was ready when this opportunity came his way.

Before he even closed on the 25 properties, John had started looking for other investors to buy some of them. Indeed, as soon as he went through the closing, he sold 15 of the properties to other investors and used the $200,000 proceeds to rehab the remaining 10. After finishing the rehab projects, he is preparing to close sales for all 10 properties and expects to realize a profit of $400,000.

Quick responses and credit readiness certainly paid off.

62. THE VALUE OF EARNEST MONEY

Sometimes earnest money means nothing, and sometimes
it means everything.

■ ■ ■

Everyone talks about doing deals on a handshake, but, in our litigious society, doing business this way is easier said than done. Nashville investor Hal Wilson has done many deals on a handshake— plus he often uses a written memo to aid everyone's memory.

On one deal, when a prospective buyer asked him how much earnest money he wanted, Hal replied, "None." That response made the man suspicious, so Hal explained his answer by saying, "If you decide next week that you don't want to buy this house from me, that's fine. I don't want you to buy it if you're not happy with it. Besides, I'd probably give the earnest money back, so I'm saving myself a trip to the bank." That said, Hal only remembers one time when a prospective buyer backed out on a deal he'd handled in this way.

Last year, a real estate agent brought Hal a prospective buyer for some duplexes. Hal gets along with almost everyone, so it was unusual that he didn't really like the buyer. He showed the buyer the duplexes that he was selling and said, "There they are. If you want to buy them, let's talk about the terms." Hal negotiated terms with the buyer and accepted a price lower than he was asking, but he asked for $1,000 in earnest money. They shook hands and the buyer even handwrote "as is" on the contract.

One week before closing, the buyer told Hal that he had revisited the properties. He requested that Hal fix a number of things in the duplexes. Hal reminded him that their terms were "as is" and that nothing about the property had changed. In fact, he had previously pointed out cracks in the foundation and noted damage from where a car had run into the house, so the buyer wouldn't be surprised. But because Hal refused to change any terms or return the $1,000 earnest money deposit, the buyer's attorney contacted him and requested he return this client's deposit. Hal told the attorney that his client's actions were made in bad faith. Hal also said that he could file an interpleader suit with a local court, turn the deposit over to the court, and let the court decide who should have it.

That proved to be a smart thing to do because, before long, the buyer dropped the matter completely.

63. PLAN FOR CONTINGENCIES

Always add contingency clauses so your purchase agreements
will cover special situations.

■ ■ ■

The first property Doug Traxler purchased didn't come with any renters, but it did come with inadequate plumbing. Before closing and while the property was still vacant, Doug decided to replace the plumbing and find new tenants. He spent money accomplishing both, then panicked because the closing got delayed and the whole deal looked questionable. Luckily, the closing did go through, and the previous owner only collected one month's rent from the new tenant that Doug had recruited.

In retrospect, Doug says he would have been better off adding contingency clauses to his purchase agreement. Specifically in this case, he should have included clauses stating that the previous owner would reimburse him for the cost of replacing the plumbing and finding new tenants. He now makes it a policy to include contingencies in all of his agreements.

64. THE PERILS OF SELLER FINANCING

If you ever take back a second mortgage, beware of extenuating circumstances. You may have to be willing to lose your money.

■ ■ ■

In 1995, Jeff and Irene Lowe (pseudonyms) had to sell their primary house because his employer was relocating from Louisville to Nashville. The Lowes listed their house for sale with a real estate agent—one whom they knew because he had previously helped them buy an investment property. They wanted to sell their Louisville residence as quickly as possible but couldn't do so before they moved. They relocated to Nashville, financed the purchase of their new home with a six-month bridge loan, and waited for their Louisville house to sell. Over the next four anxious months, the Lowes received few offers on their Louisville house and finally accepted an offer of $145,000 that involved some creative seller financing.

The buyer was able to obtain a first bank loan for $116,000, and the Lowes agreed to take back a second mortgage for $29,000. They had their doubts, and, in retrospect, they wish that they had followed their gut feelings, especially when, on their way to closing the deal, their real estate agent told them that the buyer's earnest money check had bounced (though he had made it good). But their bridge loan was almost due and they had to pay it off, so they went ahead and closed the deal—starting an 18-month nightmare.

The buyer made three timely payments on his first loan and two timely payments on the Lowes's loan. He had been a mortgage broker and had also worked as an employee for several lenders. Soon after closing on the Lowes's house, the buyer started working for the company that gave him the first loan. Within six months after closing and unbeknownst to the Lowes, he obtained another loan from his employer (the first lender) as an advance on his mortgage note, and a $10,000 loan from his girlfriend's father. Because he worked for the first lender, the buyer was somehow able to have those loans attached to the first loan. Once attached to the first loan, those loans had legal priority or claim if the buyer defaulted and would get paid first if the property was sold. The Lowes learned all this after the buyer stopped making payments and after they contacted an attorney.

The Lowes' attorney suggested that the first lender could proceed more quickly and aggressively against the buyer than they could. So, pursuant to their request, the first lender finally started foreclosure proceedings in March 1996—five months after the buyer stopped paying the Lowes. In July 1996, the buyer filed a request for a Chapter 13 reorganization bankruptcy. At that time, the Lowes learned that they only had third priority, because the buyer owed the IRS more than $40,000 in back taxes and the IRS had placed a lien on the property. In October 1996, the court granted the buyer's request and issued an order for his Chapter 13 reorganization. The buyer, however, soon stopped complying with the court order, and in December 1996, the court suspended its order at the request of the IRS.

At that time, the first lender restarted foreclosure proceedings. Then the buyer filed for Chapter 11 bankruptcy and stayed in the house until April 1997. Finally, in May 1997, the house went on the auction block.

Before the auction, Jeff contacted and successfully negotiated with the IRS for second priority on the proceeds from the sale of the house. The IRS had a 120-day right of redemption to seize the property and cover the tax lien. At auction, the first lender made a first bid and set it at $140,000 to cover its losses. During the auction, the first lender actually tried to make a deal with the Lowes but wanted too much money, and the Lowes walked away from it. The house sold for $145,000, which covered the bank's losses, but the Lowes weren't able to collect any money. The only bright side to this saga was that they could show a loss that served to reduce their tax payments that year.

65. BACKWARDS MATH

During distressed property sales, add (don't subtract) the
"deficiencies" to the amount of principal.

■ ■ ■

Investor John Lay was in the market for distressed properties—
he liked to buy them before foreclosure—when he found a decent
house in an upscale neighborhood on the market. The house had an
$80,000 first mortgage on which the owner was $12,000 behind and
a $20,000 second mortgage on which the owner was $10,000 defi-
cient. John guessed that it would take three months for him to make
$10,000 in repairs before he could sell the house. After evaluating
the market comps, he estimated that the repaired house could sell for
$140,000.

At first, John thought this looked like a good deal apart from repairs and holding costs, considering that the combined mortgages of
$100,000 minus the $12,000 and $10,000 deficiencies left a $78,000
balance. After some time and thought, though, John questioned if it
was really a good deal—even apart from repairs and holding costs.
He realized he had to base it on $100,000 *plus* the $12,000 and
$10,000 deficiencies, which produced a $122,000 balance—an amount
much too high for this deal.

Sometimes, all the numbers can get confusing. At first glance,
deficiencies may seem like reductions of the debt when, in fact, they
are part of the debt. Whoever owes on the loans also owes for any
deficiencies.

66. PUT 20 PERCENT DOWN

Don't pay for private mortgage insurance (PMI) if you can avoid
it by putting at least 20 percent down on your mortgage.

■ ■ ■

Investor Dan Auito (http://www.magicbullets.com) advises new
investors not to confuse homeowner's insurance with private mortgage insurance or PMI.

PMI protects the lender, while homeowner's insurance protects
the buyer. Dan says, "When you put down 20 percent of value on a
home's purchase in the form of a down payment, you are, in effect,
protecting the lender from yourself, because if the bank foreclosed
on you for nonpayment, it could sell the home quickly for less than
full value and still get paid in full."

■ TIPS

---

58. Use credit card financing judiciously. It can save the day—and your deal!

59. No one keeps extra money around to cover repairs and emergencies, so put some of your rental income into a reserve account.

60. Make sure you understand what government agencies like the Small Business Administration require before starting to build your dream property.

61. Develop your borrowing power so you can move quickly on big deals that come your way.

62. Sometimes earnest money means nothing and sometimes it means everything.

63. Always add contingency clauses so your purchase agreements will cover special situations.

64. If you ever take back a second mortgage, beware of extenuating circumstances. You may have to be willing to lose your money.

65. During distressed property sales, add (don't subtract) the "deficiencies" to the amount of principal.

66. Don't pay for private mortgage insurance (PMI) if you can avoid it by putting at least 20 percent down on your mortgage.

PART 4

CAUTIONARY
MEASURES

■ ■ ■

Most successful real estate investors know that real estate investing is a business that involves many complex issues and requires professional skills and experience.

First, you must operate your business in its optimal form as a trustee, partner, stockholder, or member of a business entity. Unfortunately, business entities have many special legal and tax requirements. As a result, you'll probably have to rely on the skills and experiences of legal and accounting professionals to meet those requirements.

When you work on your properties, you have to do everything safely and legally. Otherwise, future tenants could be harmed, and you or future investors could be sued, fined, or even jailed. That means you'll have to rely on the skills and experiences of licensed contractors, skilled laborers, and city codes inspectors. To be prepared for anything and everything, be willing to work with qualified professionals.

Once again, successful real estate investors realize that real estate investing is a numbers game, so successful real estate investors usually develop excellent negotiation skills. They quickly and carefully collect and analyze information about real estate opportunities, then negotiate their best possible deals. Sometimes they pay a bit more than they'd like to so they can make more money in the future.

With that in mind, remember to treat deals as unemotional business opportunities. When negotiations fail, don't agonize. Simply move on to the next one. When negotiations succeed, arrange to have a timely closing and, perhaps, file your contract in the real estate title records. Promptly prepare for the closing by ordering and delivering proof of property insurance to your closing officer. Then, after you close the deal, go through a follow-up process. Make sure that all necessary paperwork has been filed within a reasonable time. And take time to reward or otherwise thank everyone involved in the transaction.

Some situations, though, can be totally outrageous and unpredictable (as in many of the following stories). Successful landlords have learned to roll with the punches.

If you keep your wits—and sense of humor—about you, you can survive and thrive, too.

If I were to submit my own "cautionary measure" story in this book, this is what I would include. All investors who use computer technology can relate to this one!

When Rob Hill first started collecting stories for this book, he decided to use the Internet to contact as many active investors as possible. He first developed a Web site at http://www.RealEstateStories.com. Then he decided to collect e-mail addresses so he could contact active investors and tell them about his Web site and his book. Over several weeks, he accumulated a database of approximately 500 active investors. Then, because he did not know all of the investors he was contacting, he drafted an e-mail letter in compliance with the federal CAN-SPAM act.

Then one Tuesday morning, he downloaded and tried out several new free bulk e-mailing software programs. He tried all of the freeware by sending test e-mails to himself. Once he determined the "best" choice, he sent an introductory e-mail to each of the investors in his database. It took about 45 minutes to send all of those e-mails.

Next, he drafted a second e-mail and attached a blank story submission form to it. Because he had to attend a meeting, he decided to let the freeware automatically send the second e-mails. He started the freeware and left for his meeting. Three hours later, Rob returned to his home and checked his computer to see if all the e-mails had been properly sent. To his great surprise, he discovered that the freeware was still sending the e-mails. Well, he figured that the second e-mails might take a bit longer because they had a sizable attachment—but three hours seemed a bit long.

Uh oh. He looked more closely at the freeware and realized that it was in a send loop. It had sent the e-mails *repeatedly*. He stopped the program immediately and tried to figure out what had happened. Was it a bug in the freeware? Was there a virus on his computer? He wasn't sure.

Over the next few days, Rob received numerous complaints from e-mail recipients. Several people received several copies of the second mail and were quite upset about it. Nonetheless, he sent apologies to all those who complained and chose not to contact all the other recipients. In a welcome demonstration of understanding, many of those who complained eventually shared their real estate investment stories with him.

To this day, Rob doesn't know why the freeware malfunctioned, but he's grateful for the patience and forgiving nature of those who received his e-mails. The results? You're reading them in this book.

67. BEWARE OF CHANGING RULES AND REGULATIONS

Check laws and regulations before you start land development,
plus check them as the job continues because they can change
at any time. Also, be prepared for any government-related
approvals to take four times longer than you planned.

■ ■ ■

Before his first crash course in land development, Detroit native Larry Elliott was a member of Ford Motor's GT racecar team, racing champion automobiles on tracks across America. In addition, he owned part of a farm in central Tennessee that one of his ancestor's had received for fighting in the War of 1812. Because Larry had always felt an affinity for land, he decided to leave Ford in the early 1970s to develop and operate his own hunting and fishing campgrounds, complete with a marina.

In 1973, Larry found an ideal location: an 80-acre parcel of country land on the edge of Saginaw Bay, Michigan. He met with a local bank president and learned that the bank would be happy to help him with temporary loans to buy the land, even though it was his first commercial venture. Bank officers suggested he apply for a permanent loan through the Small Business Administration (SBA). Meanwhile, because the SBA application and approval process would take a long time, they gave him a construction loan so he could start developing the land.

Not all was smooth sailing in this project, and Larry faced several time-consuming setbacks. For example, he had drafted a septic system, then gotten a government inspector's approval and had it installed perfectly. However, the second (and final) inspector rejected the already-installed septic system and ordered Larry to move it 300 feet to the middle of the campgrounds near the campfire sites.

Larry had also drafted a boat canal and started dredging it from his planned marina location to Saginaw Bay. Before he got too far, a Michigan Department of Natural Resources inspector stopped the process, because regulations said it needed to lie parallel to the water's edge. Larry imagined that his only choice would be to dig a new canal to meet these requirements. But he kept his machines working—and fortunately found an old, overgrown canal lying perpendicular to the water's edge of Saginaw Bay! He was able to rebuild this canal to suit the requirements.

Larry also built a hunting and fishing lodge at the center of the campgrounds and cut a 20-foot swath through the thick woods from that building to the road. The lodge needed power, so the electric company service dropped by to install service. That's when he was told he had to cut a much bigger, 60-foot path for them to work. Undaunted, he hired a bulldozer to cut a wider swath through the woods.

After more delays, Larry finally opened the resort and, for two years, enjoyed leading hunting and fishing tours. Unfortunately, his business was still floating on temporary bank loans because he'd never been able to arrange a permanent loan—in part because no one told him to get a letter of commitment *before* starting to build. The SBA had turned down Larry's request for a loan because the construction was almost complete.

It seemed as though nothing was going Larry's way. During that time, worldwide oil supplies were being embargoed and inflation was skyrocketing. Consequently, he was paying 17 percent interest on a $140,000 loan balance. So in the mid-70s, he sold his hunting, fishing, and marina development to private investors. Luckily, he walked away from his very first commercial deal with a tidy profit and a lot of education—especially about the rules and lead times needed for loans, inspections, and government requirements.

As a side note, although Larry moved to Tennessee in 1978, his son stayed in Michigan and has since established himself as a reputable commercial developer.

68. APPEARANCES CAN FOOL YOU!

Sellers aren't always the people they appear to be.

■ ■ ■

Investor Kim Sandell had spoken with a man about buying his house but soon discovered that it was in foreclosure. The man appeared neat, nice, and well spoken, yet strange. He had filled his house with auto parts—no furniture, just auto parts.

Once she learned about his pending foreclosure, Kim decided not to buy from him at that time but kept track of him and left his information in her files. She was happy to learn that the man was able to avoid foreclosure on his house but felt sad when she later saw the house go into foreclosure once again. She was saddened, that is, until she read in the newspaper that this neat, nice, well-spoken man had just been arrested for allegedly murdering a neighbor!

69. LAND SURVEYS TELL ALL

To make sure that the house you want to buy is physically located on the land that you're buying, order a survey and title search before you make a purchase.

■ ■ ■

Twelve siblings had recently inherited a large farm and subdivided it to sell in smaller units. Vicki Bianchi agreed to buy a house that was located on one acre of this farm. Ever the cautious buyer, she ordered a survey of "her" house and yard. She observed that the lot had to be 240 feet square or the house couldn't really fit on it.

Indeed, the lot simply wasn't big enough. Because she discovered the discrepancy long before closing, she was able to cancel the deal and walk away without incurring costs other than the survey. A few hundred dollars saved her thousands more and freed her resources for better deals.

70. RUN THE NUMBERS BUT TRUST YOUR INTUITION

Trust your intuition or gut feeling and things will usually
work out better.

■ ■ ■

Nancy Spivey is a real estate investor, speaker, and business coach in Atlanta, Georgia. From a family chock full of entrepreneurs, Nancy has an open mind for growing new businesses. Her grandfather, an uncle, and other members of her family have been investing in real estate for many years, so Nancy grew up in the business. In fact, she regularly spent childhood Sundays following up on real estate For Sale classified listings. She has been an active investor for many years, but has lost sleep over only one deal—the one in which she failed to follow her gut feeling.

In the late 1990s, Atlanta was regarded as the "Silicon Valley of the South." Local software and hardware technology businesses were all booming and the population was growing. With so much money and so many buyers available, real estate prices skyrocketed. Because Atlanta is also home to the more than 3,100 members of the Georgia Real Estate Investors Association (Georgia REIA), the environment really pressed investors to find good deals.

Nancy found what looked like an especially good deal under the circumstances: a duplex with a large living room and dining room combination on each side, located in one of Atlanta's burgeoning south-side neighborhoods. With such a strong demand for single-family residences, though, it made sense to convert the duplex into a large, four-bedroom, two-bath, single-family residence. She contacted members of her investment team and calculated repair costs. The numbers looked good, everyone said it sounded great, and Nancy thought she could make some money. But her "gut" told her otherwise. She slept poorly when she thought about the deal, even before she actually completed it.

Over her many years as a successful investor, Nancy avoided deals that felt wrong to her. This time, all the numbers and advisors suggested going forward, so she bought the duplex and hired two contractors to rehab it. Soon after the work started, the contractors stopped showing up. Nancy asked around, but no one seemed to know where they were. Then, a week later, she received a call from one of the contractor's mothers. The contractors had been caught stealing from other jobsites; they would be in jail for a while. Nancy was stuck, so she went to the hardware store to purchase supplies. She had to get the work done.

As she loaded her pickup truck, two urban cowboys named "Rob" and "Bob" saddled up to her and said, "Howdy, little lady . . . looks like you could use some help. We're new to town, but we do good work." Nancy sure needed help so she hired them on the spot. The urban cowboys quickly completed her rehab work.

When they were finished, the old duplex had been transformed into a beautiful single-family residence and it looked great, both inside and outside. It featured new light fixtures, new carpet, refinished tiles, and an updated heating and air-conditioning system. Nancy found a mother and daughter, Section 8 tenants, who wanted to move in as soon as possible. For almost a year, things seemed to go great. Then Nancy learned that the mother had developed drug and alcohol problems; Section 8 authorities were removing them from the home immediately. When Nancy inspected her beautiful house, she discovered that the mother and daughter had been fighting. They'd broken windows and trashed the place. Their security deposit was, of course, insufficient to cover all the damages and Nancy had to rehab her beautiful house once more.

After she found and hired a qualified contractor for the second round of renovations, she gave him a key and he apparently went to work. A week or so later, when Nancy stopped by to check his progress, she noticed that he had moved a lot of household items into the place. He quickly explained that he'd had to move out of his previous abode, that he really liked her beautiful house and wanted to rent it. She told him that he would have to apply and qualify, just like anyone else. He didn't, though, and since she had given him a key to the house, she had to formally evict him in court. As soon as she evicted him, Nancy decided she'd had enough and sold the house. After holding costs and double the rehabbing costs, her profit on this house was small.

In retrospect, Nancy wishes she hadn't done the deal at all. She says, "I'd never regretted a deal that I *didn't* do, but this is one deal I sure regret doing." From that time forward, though, she would always trust her God-given gift—her intuition.

71. TALK OVER YOUR PLANS WITH NEIGHBORS

Draw your neighbors into your building plans and ask for their support on any variance issues.

■ ■ ■

Like many wise real estate agents, Doug Simpson has started investing in real estate. Early last year, Doug purchased what he describes as a "shanty" near Sylvan Park, a popular, high-growth area in Nashville, Tennessee. The shanty measured all of 21 feet by 27 feet. It had a tin roof, no electrical service, and a water line that wasn't hooked up. When he paid $33,000 for it, Doug thought he could update, rehab, and sell it for between $80,000 and $100,000. After all, four town home-style condominiums had just been built on a neighboring lot and sold for $129,000 each.

Doug brought his tools over to the shanty and, for a few months, started updating and rehabbing it. Unfortunately, he had to travel out of town on business, so his work went slowly. But it went even more slowly after someone broke into his tool trailer and stole $6,000 worth of tools.

Around that time, a city codes inspector inspecting the new condominiums stopped by to look at the shanty. Although Doug was only doing simple work, he was working without permits, so the city codes inspector cited him. He felt really demoralized by this, but then he heard some good news.

A local developer announced plans to build 15 craftsman-style, custom bungalow houses just down the street from Doug's shanty. Those bungalows would make stylish additions to the neighborhood, and they would fetch between $140,000 and $225,000. So Doug decided that, rather than rehab and update his shanty, he would build a nice house with a carriage house on his lot. First, he would build the carriage house and then, once it was finished, he would live in the upstairs suite while he razed the shanty and built his own craftsman-styled bungalow. He started on his carriage house with cedar shake, timber brackets, and hardy plank siding.

To comply with city codes, Doug started to build the carriage house where it could someday be attached to the beautiful bungalow that he planned to build. City codes also required, though, that building structures be placed at specific minimum distances, or setbacks, from the road and other property boundaries. When Doug got started, he built the carriage house just beyond the residential setback but inside the garage setback. He could use the carriage house as a garage, but for use as a garage, city codes required that he build it no taller than 16 feet.

Unfortunately, it's hard to build a two-story building lower than 16 feet—unless the floors are small and the roof is flat. That meant Doug would need a variance to build his craftsman-styled carriage house with a regular-sized garage and a useful apartment above it. When he petitioned for a zoning variance and when his petition was heard, his neighbors all opposed this idea.

Since that hearing, Doug has talked in depth with his neighbors and explained what he was planning to do. They apologized, said that they hadn't understood his intentions, and told him that they wouldn't oppose his petition if he applied again. Doug had to make a decision, though—time is money, and it would take several months to get another hearing, so he decided to scrap his plan and make his carriage house just a garage.

Unfortunately, because he hadn't explained his plans to his neighbors, the neighborhood lost a potentially beautiful addition, and Doug lost time and money.

72. BE A WISE CONSUMER OF INSURANCE

Insure your properties with policies that will cover all
contingencies, including lost income.

■ ■ ■

Ted and Mary Peterson (pseudonyms) started investing in real estate while living in Louisville, Kentucky. When they later moved 220 miles south to Nashville, Tennessee, the Petersons hired a local real estate agent to manage their Louisville properties. Most of their family and many of their friends still lived in Louisville, though, so the Petersons frequently returned to visit. When they visited, they often inspected their properties, and during one visit, they noticed something especially unusual.

In the front yard of their English Tudor duplex was an extremely large oak tree—so large that, where its trunk met the ground, the trunk had a seven-foot diameter. Five feet above the ground, its diameter was still wide at 4.5 feet. The tree was magnificent, but its root systems had caused some damage to the driveway next door, and the neighbor had needed to cut the roots so he could repair the broken pavement. Unfortunately, when he cut the roots, he weakened the tree's support.

In October 1998, an unusually severe storm front moved through Louisville and took down a lot of trees—including this massive oak tree. When the tree blew over, the main trunk crashed into the second story of the duplex. A limb with a diameter of 12 inches stopped the tree from falling all the way through the building. It destroyed the roof and severely damaged the upstairs living room and bedroom.

Ted happened to be in town when the storms hit, and a kind neighbor called and told him about the damage. As a result, he was able to come and supervise early repairs on the home. He negotiated with the insurance adjustor, specified repair materials and labor with the contractors, and stressed his desire to restore the duplex in an authentic way. Unfortunately, as soon as he left, things went awry, and he had to follow up repeatedly with everyone involved from a distance.

In the end, the total damages amounted to $80,000—more than one third of the property's $235,000 fair market value. Fortunately, the Petersons carried good insurance policies that covered loss of rents as well as repairs; they just had to follow up with diligence to make sure all details of the repair went smoothly.

73. LIABILITY INSURANCE IS A NECESSITY FOR LANDLORDS

Maintain liability insurance to cover property owners and managers, because tenants can sue for the strangest reasons.

■ ■ ■

When you own or manage a large number of properties, you own or manage a large amount of risk. Insurance helps people in similar situations diffuse their risk and gets them out of tough legal situations at times. Maintaining the right amounts and types of insurance is well advised, especially when it involves tenant liability issues.

Experienced Nashville investor Hal Wilson manages a large number of properties, so he maintains a large amount of insurance. As Hal's experiences show, paying large insurance premiums for this coverage is worth every penny he spends.

Many years ago, one of Hal's tenants decided in the middle of deep-frying a meal that she needed to go to the store. She asked her daughter to keep an eye on the grease, saying that she'd be right back. The daughter, who was busy talking on the phone, only half listened to her mom and kept on talking—until she saw flames shooting up in the kitchen. In a panic, she ran and got her next-door neighbor to help her put out the fire. The neighbor raced into the kitchen and picked up the blazing pan with her bare hand. Scalding grease sloshed back on her arms and burned her badly. She dropped the pan and scalding grease splashed everywhere, burning her even more. Someone finally called the fire department. The firefighters arrived, put the fire out, and took the neighbor to the hospital.

Soon after that incident, Hal's tenants sued him for $1 million. They claimed that he had installed a defective stove and that it had overheated. Hal's insurance company defended his position and arranged to settle the claim out of court for much less than $1 million.

Another time, one of Hal's tenants called him from the hospital. She claimed that being in the hospital was his fault because she had fallen down defective attic steps in the rental home. Hal wasn't sure what to make of her argument until he visited her and saw her in person. He quickly deduced that her boyfriend beat her on a regular basis. In the meantime, her father had come to town, and she needed an excuse for her serious bruises. She decided to blame her condition on the "rent man" and sued Hal for $500,000. Hal's insurance company defended him and got an out-of-court settlement for $35,000.

Given these kinds of situations, landlords and managers can't afford to ignore insurance issues. The amount you pay for insurance premiums could pay for itself many times over.

74. GETTING THE RIGHT INSURANCE COVERAGE

If you're an investor who builds houses, know what your
insurance covers, and be sure to purchase
completed operations insurance.

■ ■ ■

Hal Wilson fishes in many ponds—or at least that's the analogy that he uses to describe his real estate investing. Over the years, he has invested in the "foreclosure" pond, the "fix 'n flip" pond, the "house-moving" pond, and the "house-building" pond, among others.

As a fisherman in the house-building pond, Hal partnered with an active general contractor and built a new house on a vacant lot that he owned in the Sylvan Heights area of Nashville, Tennessee. Hal contributed land and building funds to the partnership, and the contractor supervised all construction. The partners quickly built and sold a 900-square-foot cottage. It cost them $50,000 to construct, and they sold it for $60,000, for a profit of $5,000 apiece. The arrangement proved to be profitable—for a while at least.

Within a year after the cottage sold, 15 people had assembled on the deck behind the house and the deck collapsed. Apparently, no one had correctly attached the deck to the structure of the house, and three necessary 59-cent lag bolts were missing. One of the guests who fell when the deck collapsed sued Hal and his partner, claiming serious injury and total disability. His lawsuit was for $1.5 million in damages. As a result, Hal's partner had to file bankruptcy.

During the depositions that followed filing the lawsuit, Hal stated that he "and his partner" had built the deck. When representatives from his insurance company heard that, they jumped in and seized an opportunity to deny Hal coverage. They pointed out that his policy excluded partnership work and, besides, he didn't have completed operations insurance. Completed operations insurance would have protected Hal, as a builder and contractor, from liability for improper construction or installation of materials.

In effect, Hal's insurance company bailed out on him. He eventually settled the lawsuit out of court for $60,000, so he lost $55,000 on the deal. Today, he would advise other investors who fish in the home-building pond to get completed operations insurance and avoid paying out on claims such as this one.

75. DON'T EVER SKIP INSPECTIONS

Be sure to order professional property inspections before closing on a property.

■ ■ ■

John Rezvanpour and his wife Mercedes have been active in Atlanta real estate circles for a few decades. John was originally trained as a civil engineer but, for more than 15 years, has been a residential builder and investor, while Mercedes is a Realtor and serves several investor clients.

Just a few years ago, John bought an 1,850-square-foot, four-bedroom, three-bathroom ranch house on 1.1 acres in east Cobb County, a high-dollar area in metro Atlanta. Ten other investors bid against John for this house. When all was said and done, John won the bidding and the property. He skipped the inspection stage, closed on it quickly, and started rehabbing it.

As his work crews started making progress, John noticed that something—quite literally—stunk. Whenever more workers were present, the stench in the air grew even stronger. Then they realized that the smell increased whenever workers flushed the toilets. That started their search for the underlying problem, and, before long, they discovered that someone had stolen (or removed and not re-placed) the house's septic tank. John originally thought it would cost $15,000 to rehab this house, but putting in a replacement septic tank cost him an additional $8,000.

Yes, even investors with years of experience can't know and fore-see all problems. That's why getting an inspector involved every time is critical.

In another situation, Charles Benn and his wife found a three-bedroom, one-bathroom house in West Philadelphia through a co-worker. It was the first house they walked through as investors. They thought that, at a buying price of $25,000, it would be worth pursu-ing as a rental, because houses in that neighborhood were selling for $45,000 to $50,000.

He says, "Because we were new to real estate investing, we thought it would be a good idea to get a home inspection along with a termite inspection. Well, thank God we did. I was with the home inspector on the second floor when the termite inspector came up and said he was finished doing his inspection. But he warned us, 'Be careful of the cat skeleton under the basement stairs.'"

Because it was around Halloween, Charles thought the termite guy was joking. But when he went into the basement with the home inspector for a final look, they realized it wasn't a joke. They saw a real cat skeleton under the basement stairs. Better to find it now rather than later!

76. BEWARE WHEN ENTERING "VACANT" PROPERTIES

"Vacant" and "abandoned" houses aren't always found
to be as advertised. Use caution when entering them
and don't go in by yourself.

■ ■ ■

Hal Wilson has been a real estate investor for four decades and has established a large referral network. Several years ago, he received a call from a man that he had known for some time. The man hoped that Hal would buy an abandoned house that he was selling on D.B. Todd Drive in Nashville, Tennessee. Hal was familiar with the address and neighborhood, and because it sounded like a deal, he headed over to check it out. The house's windows were boarded up, so he entered through the back door. The house was dark—little light could make it through the boards—so he went inside carrying a flashlight. He walked through each room and noted that trash was scattered everywhere. Then he arrived at one room with a closed door. He pushed the door open, entered slowly, and was greeted by the clenched teeth of two growling Doberman Pinschers.

Hal doesn't quite remember what happened next. In his next memory, he sees himself sitting in his truck trembling. He does remember that one of the dogs was black and the other was brown. He also knows that he has seldom, if ever, been more scared. Not surprisingly, he didn't buy the house.

On another occasion, Hal had stumbled upon squatters living in a supposedly vacant property. As he walked through the front door of this house, a heroin addict stood up and walked past him out the same door. He still had a needle dangling from his arm.

Another time, Hal had walked into the bedroom of a house on Forrest Avenue and surprised its unofficial resident. Startled, both

men jumped up and ran in opposite directions. The technically homeless man took off out the bedroom window and ran down the alley.
Hal ran out the front door, jumped into his truck, and drove away.

On yet another occasion, Hal and a longtime assistant went to inspect a house that he had just purchased. Shortly after they entered
it, a man followed them through the front door and asked, "Why are
you in my house?" Hal told this squatter that he now owned the
house and the man replied, "Well, you can't have it." Hal insisted
that he owned it and told him to leave immediately. The man shook
his head, walked out, and returned to his "home" in the crawlspace
underneath the house. Hal eventually had to board up the crawlspace
to "evict" this homeless man.

Over the years, Hal has become more cautious about avoiding
bad situations. Today, while he sometimes carries a concealed pistol
and has a permit to do so, he generally won't enter a vacant or abandoned house by himself.

77. WHEN LONG-TERM RENTERS HAVE TOO MUCH CONTROL

Don't let long-term renters limit prospective buyers' ability
to view your property.

■ ■ ■

In 1998, Sid and Rita Johnson (pseudonyms) found a "bargain"
property on the edge of one of America's wealthiest zip codes. The
building was custom built as a large duplex: one side had three bedrooms and two bathrooms; the other had two bedrooms and two-and-
a-half bathrooms. When the original owners had moved out of the
duplex, they'd rented the larger unit to a married couple who had
lived there continuously for the past 25 years. During that time,
many different people had rented the smaller unit.

When the owners decided to sell the duplex at a list price of $260,000, they had difficulty showing it. First, the unit occupied by the married couple had never been painted or updated. Second, this couple would only allow real estate agents to show their part of the duplex on weekdays between 9:00 AM and 2:00 PM. Because of this restriction, the duplex was only viewed three times during its six-month listing.

After Sid and Rita saw the duplex, they made a lowball offer of $180,000. The owner presented a counter offer at $240,000, but that was much more than Sid and Rita wanted to pay so they let it go. One month later, their real estate agent received a call from the owner's agent saying the owner would welcome another offer. They eventually negotiated a $200,000 selling price.

What's remarkable is that, in such an affluent neighborhood, Sid and Rita were able to buy an investment property for 77 percent of its list price, because the tenants effectively controlled access to viewing the property. Today, the fair market value of that duplex—if it were converted to a single-family house—would be approximately $500,000.

78. SET ASIDE FUNDS FOR POSSIBLE LEGAL ACTIONS

Be prepared to defend your actions—in court if necessary.

■ ■ ■

Several years ago, investor Hal Wilson rented a house to a married couple who, later, allowed their grown daughter to move in with them. The couple proved to be good tenants, but they eventually moved out—without taking their daughter with them. The daughter called Hal and said she intended to stay in the house. Hal told her she needed to visit his office and complete an application, and, if everything looked good, then she could certainly stay.

Well, she never came to his office, but she did invite a lot of dope smokers to move in with her. Because she was being difficult and had never been listed on the lease, Hal regarded her as a trespasser. So one afternoon, Hal and one of his assistants went over to the house and moved all of its contents to the front yard. When he returned to his office, he called a trash removal service and had a dumpster placed in front of the house.

When the daughter returned to the house and saw all her possessions strewn out on the front lawn beside a dumpster, she called and asked Hal what he was doing. He told her that, when he had some free time, he was coming over to throw everything away.

Soon after that incident, Hal received a call from her very inexperienced lawyer. Her lawyer confirmed Hal's intention and then assured Hal that they would "go to court on this one." Hal replied that that was fine with him. As a matter of fact, he told the lawyer that, as soon as they hung up, he intended to call his bank and move $10,000 from his savings account into his defense account. He said, "I have to pay my lawyers, and as soon as that $10,000 runs out, I'll transfer another $10,000. I'll beat you on this issue, no ifs, ands, or buts about it." Not surprisingly, when Hal drove by the house that evening, all of the daughter's possessions had disappeared.

On another occasion, Hal bought a duplex that sported a decrepit Volkswagen Beetle in the driveway. While the Beetle had been sitting there rusting, a medium-sized tree had grown beside the engine block and even through the hood. Hal had the tree cut down and the Beetle removed.

A short time later, the man who owned the Beetle and had previously lived in the duplex sued Hal for $1,000. The man had a new job and needed to use his Beetle to get to work. He claimed that Hal had dealt with his Beetle incorrectly.

Hal showed the judge photos of the Beetle with the tree growing through it, and the judge still awarded the man $500. In all, Hal spent $3,000 of the funds he'd set aside defending himself. He finally won the case on an appeal judgment.

79. FORECLOSURE BRINGS SURPRISES

Know how to identify the investment home you purchased
at auction to avoid having to break into it.

■ ■ ■

In 2003, John Harris (a pseudonym) paid $84,000 at the fore-
closure sale of a house that he thought would sell for $170,000 after
it was rehabbed. Apparently, the previous owner had owned the
house free and clear and then took out a home equity loan in 1999.
When that owner stopped making loan payments in early 2003, the
lender foreclosed on the house.

The house sits in a small court with three other houses, just off
a main state highway. All three houses could use a bit of work, but
the house at the center of the court really looked bad or—as many
investors joke—it suffered from a lot of deferred maintenance. After
John won the auction, he sent his check to the court and received a
deed that he filed in the courthouse. Then he headed out to inspect
his property, take photographs for insurance purposes, and start
cleaning up. When he arrived, he circled the house, took some photos and, because all of the doors and windows were locked, broke a
window to get inside the house.

Inside, the house was a mess, with clothes and furniture strewn
everywhere. John decided to contact the previous occupants as soon
as possible to see if they wanted to collect their items, so he checked
the mailbox for letters with forwarding addresses. He found that all
the letters were addressed to the local leader of the National Association for the Advancement of Colored People (NAACP), living at
2410 ABC Street. John panicked. Because the houses on the court
weren't clearly numbered, he had come into the wrong house. He
had bought 2412 ABC Street at auction. He'd just broken into a
community leader's house! He quickly put the mail back and left.

Next, John looked closely but cautiously at the other two houses on the court and finally found a mailbox almost hidden behind a bush in front of the nicer house of the two. He peeked at the mail inside and discovered—whew—that this was the right house.

He knocked on the door, and an 82-year-old retired black gentleman answered. He seemed friendly enough and asked John how he could help him—several times. John tried to explain that he now owned the house and that he wanted to look around inside. The man didn't seem to understand. Nonetheless, he invited John in and asked him to "sit a spell." John did sit down and talked with the man, who was obviously suffering from Alzheimer's.

The man showed John photos from his youth that hung on the wall. Some of the photos were evidently from World War II, when the man, much younger, was dressed as a soldier and sporting many decorations. But today, this man couldn't remember anything about the photos.

In other photos, the man wore a nice suit and a big smile, showing that he enjoyed work and the company of his coworkers. But now he couldn't remember where he had worked. He did know that he was divorced, though, and that his family had stopped talking with him since the divorce, especially because he'd allowed a younger woman to move in with him. John correctly surmised that she'd helped him cash his pension and his social security checks, but she hadn't helped him pay his loan. The doors to her bedroom and bathroom were locked, so John couldn't inspect them.

When John returned to the home he'd just bought, he tried to find contact information for the man's family. Eventually, he found a phone number for the man's brother and called him. The brother was only half-surprised to hear from John. It seemed that ever since his brother had "taken up with that Jezebel," the family had been waiting for something like this to happen. The brother and other members of the family pretty much blew off John's concerns. Because he'd paid off the man's mortgage loan and didn't think the man could pay him back, John regrettably had to file an eviction suit.

That's when the man's family came to his aid by hiring an attorney to defend him. In light of the circumstances, John thinks that the family wanted only to protect the man's equity so that they could inherit it. The man's attorney argued *pro bono* that the man was mentally incompetent at the time that he took out his home equity loan. The man (and his family) lost the case and started to appeal the decision, until they realized that hiring an appellate attorney would be expensive. Sadly, not long afterward, the man moved into a veteran's nursing home, and John could begin rehabbing his new investment home—the right one.

80. A CRUEL APRIL FOOL'S DAY JOKE

Always research title issues and buy title insurance
to cover any surprises.

■ ■ ■

For Nancy and Ned Smith (their pseudonyms), one particular property on Old Hickory Road became the April Fool's Day joke of their investment portfolio.

The saga began at a Real Estate Investors of Nashville (REIN) meeting, where Nancy picked up information that featured descriptions for 68 properties being auctioned off. An out-of-state auctioneer would be auctioning them one at a time on behalf of a real estate investment trust.

Several times, Ned and Nancy rode by one of the properties to be auctioned before the auction date, and Ned even got a chance to preview it. Their analyses suggested that this 2,600-square-foot home would be a good investment, as it was currently being leased for $1,850 a month.

On the day of the auction, most bidders fell out quickly and left Ned bidding against one other couple in $1,000 increments. The other couple, who wanted it badly, ran the bidding up until Ned got the winning bid at $180,000. Including the buyer's premium, Ned and Nancy actually paid a total of $199,000—$1,000 below the limit they had set. Based on its location, square footage, and other features, the Smiths thought they could easily turn around and sell it for $235,000, which it appraised for. This would translate into $36,000 of built-in equity on this Old Hickory property.

Then on April 1, 2000, after a long day of rehabbing another property, Ned and Nancy returned home to find an answering machine message from their Old Hickory tenants. They were asking why black plastic sheeting was connecting wooden stakes across their yard just a few yards from their front door.

The Smiths immediately drove out to the house and, in the darkness of early evening, tried to figure out what was going on. Apparently that morning, the state department of transportation had posted signs about the new road-widening project underway. Early the next morning, Ned and Nancy started making calls, checked title records, and tried to figure out what was going on.

Much to their dismay, they discovered that, shortly before listing it with the auctioneer, the previous owner had removed the title from the trust and then sold the first 60 feet of the house's front yard to the state of Tennessee for $125,000. In fact, the previous owner had pocketed all of the $125,000.

Ned and Nancy immediately contacted a real estate attorney to see if they could claim any of the money from the $125,000 sale. The attorney told them they couldn't, so they contacted another real estate attorney for a second opinion. The second attorney also confirmed that they couldn't collect any of the money, explaining that this was the best case of legally sufficient "failure to disclose" that he'd seen in 20 years of practice. They had been snookered by a real expert!

Interestingly, this property had originally been part of a real estate investment trust. To sell it, the trustee had taken the property out of the trust, sold most of the front yard to the state, and then put it back into the trust. The map and disclosure information that the auctioneer distributed appeared accurate and complete but, in retrospect, was quite vague.

Today, after three years and several delays, the state has almost finished its road-widening project. Unfortunately, to keep the property rented, Ned and Nancy had to hire a property management company and incrementally lower the monthly rent from $1,850 to $1,150. To keep their tenants happy, they had to cater promptly to every call and complaint.

During innumerable sleepless nights, they have continued to analyze what went wrong with this deal. Wrestling with unkind thoughts about the seller, they quietly hoped he'd invested his ill-gotten gains into dot-com stocks that had proven to be worthless.

81. AN INAPPROPRIATE TRADE-OUT OFFER

Keep your moral scruples about you when dealing with tenants.

■ ■ ■

John Stevens (a pseudonym) started his investing career while working as a real estate agent. Like most investors, one of his earliest investments was a single-family residence. He and his wife bought a three-bedroom, one-and-a-half-bathroom home that had been occupied for the previous four years by a Section 8 mother and her 16-year old daughter. Under the terms of their rental agreement, the government automatically paid $250 of the monthly rent, and the mother had to pay the $100 balance.

This stable investment property seemed perfect for new landlords. Then, nine months into their lease, the mother missed a payment. John and his wife, in their early 20s, had no experience as landlords, and they had no fellow investors to turn to for advice.

They naively let their tenants slide on the rent for a month. Then their tenant missed another month's rent, so John went over to the house alone to speak with her.

When he arrived, their tenant invited him to sit for a while. He listened while she explained that she had no money, times were really tough, and she couldn't do anything about paying the rent. She had tried. John then explained how he needed her rent to pay the mortgage. If she didn't pay him, he couldn't pay the lender, and the lender would foreclose on the house. They would all lose. The tenant either didn't understand or didn't care. She ignored his explanation and proposed another arrangement. She said that her daughter was upstairs in her bedroom. John rolled his eyes in surprise, stood up, and promptly walked out.

Ten years later, John ran into the grown, 26-year old daughter at a local mall. He didn't remember her, but she remembered him. She asked how everything was and gave no indication that she knew about her mother's proposal. For a million different moral and legal reasons, John was glad he had walked out.

82. KNOW WHAT YOU BUY—INSIDE AND OUT

What looks good on the outside could be a cesspool
on the inside.

■ ■ ■

Several years ago, John Main (a pseudonym) went to his local courthouse steps and bought a house for $15,001. The house was a three-bedroom, one-and-a-half bath ranch measuring 1,250 square feet. John estimated that it was worth $92,000 fixed up.

The first lender had foreclosed on the owners' $15,000 loan, so when John won the auction, he wiped out the second lender's mortgage and "stole" the house for $1 over the amount of the debt. Normally, that would be considered a good deal, but John was concerned. Why didn't the second lender and other auction-goers bid on this house? He had previewed it and, before the closing, driven by it again and observed that the exterior looked fine, though he couldn't go inside because it was occupied. Surprised to be the only bidder, his surprise grew when he finally went inside the house.

The tenant and her children had totally trashed it. The plumbing had backed up and the sink was full of spoiled, rotting food. The kitchen floor was covered with trash, too, except where standing water had rotted though the floor and into the basement. Strange cultures and insects scuttled, scurried, and thrived everywhere. The toilets, the sinks, the bathtubs, and the buckets and trash bags that littered the house were full of human excrement. The walls and floors were sticky, brown, and fuzzy. The plumbing had quite obviously failed them, as had the trash service. According to neighbors, the kids had dumped their excrement in the storm drains every night until the state removed them from the cesspool that was their home. Overall, everything was pretty shitty.

John hired brave souls in hazardous material (air-insulated) suits to clean the house. They were overcome many times, so they worked slowly but deliberately. John spent $30,000 to clean and repair this house. Then, two weeks before he was ready to sell it, his lender called to inform him that the discharged second lender was filing suit to rescind John's purchase. The second lender said that they never received notice of the sale, so they sued John, the first lender, and the auctioneer. Then the second lender's attorney underwent two back surgeries within a five-month period. Time dragged on as John paid the mortgage on this newly cleaned but empty house.

Months later, John's title insurance company finally obtained an order that released the house from litigation and entitled the second lender to a cash-only award. John's holding costs had skyrocketed, but he was finally free to sell the house—and finally able to free himself of this costly, unnerving situation.

83. CONFIRM YOUR AGENT'S MARKET RESEARCH

As a long-distance landlord, even if you rely on trusted agents
and managers, still do your own market research.

■ ■ ■

Sue Summers (a pseudonym) may just live forever. Over the
past 20 years, she has walked 5 miles every day. Not only has this
been good for her health, but she's also stumbled onto good real
estate investment deals.

In 1994, while walking in the Highlands area of Louisville, Kentucky, Sue spotted a "For Sale" sign in the front lawn of an attractive
two-story duplex. She looked the property over, liked it, and took
time to memorize the name of the real estate agent and his phone number. When she returned to her house, she told her husband, Michael
(also a pseudonym), about the property, and they called the agent.
Imagine everyone's surprise when he said, "Why, I just put that sign
out 30 minutes ago. And I'm still here if you want to come over and
look at the property."

Within minutes, Michael and Sue arrived. They carefully looked
at the property and wrote up an offer to buy it. Sue got to work late
that day after completing the paperwork, but she said, "It was worth
it. We bought the duplex for $125,000, and I'm pleased to say I
found a real deal 'walking for dollars.'"

In 2003, Michael and Sue decided to sell the duplex for $205,000,
because they were living in Nashville, Tennessee, and no longer
wanted to own property in Louisville. "It was time to let it go," she
said. For several years, they had been long-distance landlords and
were forced—as a practical matter—to employ the services of a local
real estate agent/property manager. They had always trusted him to
act in their best interests, so when he said that the market was slow
but that, at $205,000, they were getting fair market value for their

duplex, they believed him. Then, at the closing for this property, they were surprised to hear that the demand for duplexes was high while the supply was quite low. Learning that fact gave them reason to pause and question their agent/property manager. He had assured them that he'd checked comparable sales and that their selling price was right. But during the weeks right after that closing, they did some research and discovered that the right price was about $25,000 more than what they'd actually received for their duplex.

This good deal could have been much more lucrative if they had taken time to confirm what their agent had been telling them—and had done their own market research.

84. FORECLOSURES: YOU NEVER KNOW WHAT TO EXPECT

Walk into foreclosure situations with your eyes open and the sheriff's department at your side, if necessary.

■ ■ ■

Within the last few years (since the terrorist attacks of 9/11), Bob Madden (a pseudonym) purchased a 900-square-foot house at a foreclosure sale. Before the sale, Bob—like so many other interested investors—tried to inspect the property. But the previous owner just slammed the door in his face. And, like every other investor, he noticed the tarps that covered the roof and realized that the cost of repairs would be steep.

After Bob paid $24,000 on his winning bid and received his deed, he went to inspect the property once more. He knocked on the front door and received no answer, so he walked around back and found the previous owner walking circles on the back porch. Bob left the man alone, went around to the front, and tacked a notice on the front door. The notice declared that he had purchased the house. He then filed an eviction action shortly after and contacted the sheriff's department to serve his eviction order. When the sheriff arrived and no one answered the front door, the department hired a locksmith to break the lock and open the door.

They entered the house, looked around, and soon found the previous owner living in a tent on the back porch. The previous owner claimed that he was armed and refused to come out of his tent. The deputies drew their weapons and, after many orders and much cajoling, they finally got him to walk out of his tent. Because he seemed unstable emotionally, the sheriff's department took him into custody. Then, as they placed him in one of the police cruisers, he told them that if they went into the house, it would "go boom." The sheriff's deputies immediately evacuated it and called the city bomb squad.

When the bomb squad arrived, they entered the house and found that it was indeed wired to explode—but no explosives were connected to the wires. Members of the bomb squad grew more cautious, though, when they learned that the previous owner was an electrical engineer who had also become a chemist. In addition, he was a Vietnam veteran and a diagnosed schizophrenic.

Clearly, no one knew what to expect. Notes attached to pieces of furniture recorded their temperatures at given times of day and described the exact angle that the furniture should have with respect to the walls. Notes attached to light switches described the amperage that it took to flip them on. Notebooks recorded the weight of his coats, knives, and other odd objects at different times. Obviously, these were signs that he was desperately grasping at reality from his crazy, confused world. The authorities turned this poor guy over to his father for custody and care.

Bob discovered that the house itself was in horrible shape. Outside, tarps covered most of the roof and drained water toward strategically placed funnels. The funnels led to pipes that drained the water down to the ground surrounding the house. As a result, the house was encircled by a small, manmade moat. Bob had to hire a backhoe just to regrade the earth around the house.

Inside, roof leakage had rotted through the ceilings, the walls, and the floors. In the rear of the house near the back porch, the damage was worse. The kitchen was cram-packed with assorted items that trapped moisture, so mold and mildew were everywhere. The drywall was rotted and studs in the walls crumbled to the touch, while ceiling joists swung freely with no connection to the wall.

Before the rehab job was complete, Bob had spent $28,000 to replace the roof and decking, ceilings, floors, and walls. But at least he now owned a place that's wired for a happy family to live in—not for explosives.

85. ROSE-COLORED GLASSES DON'T SERVE YOU

Take off your rose-colored glasses when doing your due diligence.

■ ■ ■

New investor Phil Pelletier hit the streets, attempting to find people anxious to "give away" their homes due to personal circumstances (job change, divorce, etc.). He came across an individual who was in bankruptcy and wished to get out of his home and its mortgage payments. (Red flag #1: A person in bankruptcy is protected from any public filing of a notice of default.) It was a nice, newer place, 1,700 square feet with a big fenced yard. After repairs, its value was about $145,000. His latest loan statement showed that he owed $111,000. (Red flag #2: Statements of current monthly loans do not include missed payments, legal fees, or any other funds advanced on the borrower's behalf.) The loan statement also mentioned paying the property taxes on the borrower's behalf. The final nail in the coffin was the bank's automated account system, which confirmed that the mortgage holder's last payment was received in August (two months before Phil met him). Just how far could this place be behind in payments?

Says Phil, "Through my rose-colored glasses, I paid the owner $2,000 in cash for the deed based on these factors:

- No notice of default had been filed.
- Last mortgage payment had been made in August.
- Taxes had been "paid by the lender."
- $30,000 in equity for the taking on a simple quitclaim deed.

"But here's what I found out the home actually represented. The guy had not paid his mortgage in over two years; thus he owed the tidy sum of $141,000. His bankruptcy prevented any public filing of his default status into the public record. The August payment was a result of a bankruptcy court-mandated payment (the automated system shows only the last payment made). The taxes were three years behind, which I should have checked before I got involved in the home. My screw up.

"Instead, I had gone by the paperwork indicating the lender was "paying the taxes." The lender was, in fact, paying the taxes from three years before, just to keep the home from being turned over to the taxman.

"So I'm out $2,000 cash on a home that is completely underwater from a loan-to-value (LTV) perspective. I tried to offer the bank the original loan balance as a short sale. It took so long to find the right people to communicate with at the bank, the home went to the sheriff's sale five months after I first took title to it.

"In the end, I realized I had done my due diligence through rose-colored glasses. Today, I call it a $2,000 learning experience—or it could be considered a $2,000 seminar."

86. COVER YOURSELF AGAINST TITLE MIX-UPS

Always buy title insurance—even for your flips!

■ ■ ■

Mercedes Rezvanpour is a real estate agent in Atlanta, Georgia. She counts many of Atlanta's investors as her clients. Her husband, John, has been a builder and investor for more than 15 years. Together, they've been part of a lot of investment deals.

Over the last few years, Atlanta's West End neighborhood has become a hotbed for investors. John recently bought a 50-year-old, 1,800-square-foot, three-bedroom, two-bath, ranch-style house. The house was unlisted, and the owner had simply approached him while he was rehabbing a house across the street. She admitted that her house was a fixer-upper, but she only wanted $50,000 for it—all cash. Because similar houses in the neighborhood were selling for $130,000, John hoped to rehab it and sell it quickly for about $119,000.

After closing on the house, John started rehabbing it. Mercedes optimistically placed one of her For Sale signs in the front yard and put one of her key boxes on the door. Later that day, Mercedes received her first call—but not from an interested buyer. The caller asked Mercedes to move her sign and remove her key box—she claimed to own the house! Mercedes told her that she couldn't own the house because John had just bought it. He immediately called the closing attorney who promised to find out what was going on.

As it turned out, the previous owner had sold the house twice: first to the person who'd made that call and then, one month later, to John. The problem occurred because of a title mix-up: the first purchase was described in terms of its subdivision location, and the second was described in terms of its street address. John usually didn't bother buying title insurance when he purchased flippers. Luckily, for some reason, he had purchased title insurance on this one. However, the caller/first buyer had *not* purchased title insurance, so she wasn't protected from the title mix-up problem.

Although he prevailed in this case, because of the shady seller and the risk he'd encountered, John has since passed on deals in that neighborhood. But he learned a valuable lesson: he always buys title insurance to protect his purchases.

87. PROTECTION AGAINST TITLE SEARCH ERRORS

If you want a title search done right, do it yourself, or hire
a title company you trust to do it correctly.

■ ■ ■

Investor Pat Kiehl had just finished refinancing a single-family rental he'd purchased about two years before. The title search on the property revealed two liens that he thought should have been taken care of when he'd purchased it from the bank. One lien was a board-up fee from the city for about $200, and the other was a waste management fee for about $400.

Pat found out that the $200 board-up lien was recorded one month after he had made the purchase and the $400 lien hadn't been recorded at all. It was a city charge for nonpayment on the previous owner's bill before the bank took over possession. Both should have shown up on a city lien search if they had been handled properly.

Pat spoke to a representative of the underwriting firm that handled the foreclosure sale for the bank and learned that, basically, the firm only covered recorded liens. So if the lien search (which should cover local municipalities or government utility companies) got handled incorrectly, guess who has to suffer? The buyer.

In another situation, Pat had helped his handyperson purchase her first house. One year later, she decided to refinance it. A title search showed a code lien for $40,000 had been recorded by the city only one month after she'd purchased the house. She hit the roof. This lien—levied due to not having the grass cut—was accumulating at a rate of $250 a day. So she met with city representatives and asked where she might get a gun to shoot certain employees (not the thing to do around a government office nowadays). Fortunately, the representative agreed to release the lien, and she was able to refinance her home.

What an ironic contrast to Pat's situation! The city's representatives said they couldn't release the lien on his property, but they might consider waiving the interest that had accrued. "Big deal," he thought.

Where does the fault lie in this situation? Did the underwriting agents overlook the lien, or did the city not report it correctly? What Pat knows is that he's had to do the research when the bank or its agents should have already taken care of it.

If this happens to you, how can you protect yourself? First, make sure you get a copy of the lien search with your closing (or prior to the closing). Second, follow up with the local government agencies that service that location. Code violations may or may not become liens and therefore may or may not show up on the supposed lien search. You may have to call a specific local agency prior to closing and perform your own due diligence, gathering everything you can in writing.

Possible barriers can be the following:

- These agencies want to be paid for their service.
- They sometimes require ten days to do it.
- Getting government employees to put something in writing is like pulling teeth.

As a footnote, Pat came across a little-known statistic in his research—that only 7 percent of all title claims actually get paid. He concludes, "Somebody is making some serious money here, and buyers are paying for it."

88. DEALING WITH TROUBLEMAKERS

Reduce your theft troubles by not doing certain things
and not saying other things.

■ ■ ■

Some investors use a cherry-picking approach to do a select few high-profit deals. Other investors use a shotgun approach to do a large number of small-profit deals. Some find themselves doing plenty of deals in "troubled" areas, and these situations can be, well, troublesome. Experienced investors have learned to work around the troubles—all kinds.

For example, if you notice that copper plumbing on your rehabbed houses keeps disappearing, then start using PVC plumbing instead of copper. If you notice that your brand-new toilets and kitchen cabinets keep disappearing, then don't have them installed until your tenants are ready to move in. If you already have a relatively new HVAC unit and a neighbor removes it in the middle of the night, then don't replace it until the house gets occupied.

At first, such thievery may make you mad—really mad—but eventually you'll realize that, as hard as it may be to believe, thieving becomes a cost of doing business. So you can lay the groundwork, install the plumbing (PVC, of course), and run the wires, but don't install the fixtures until someone is there to look after them. Even then, you never really know for sure.

A few years ago, Hal Wilson hired a work crew to rehab a house in a troubled area. He lent the workers his tools so that they could get the job done quickly and professionally. He told these crew members the same thing he tells every other crew: take care of the tools. He always says, "When you use the port-o-lets, take the tools inside with you; don't leave them laying around outside. When you leave the job site, lock the tools inside the building—preferably, in a closet." Whenever his crews followed those simple rules, things usually worked out well.

As far as he could tell, this particular crew was following the rules. Then one day, Hal stopped by the job site and one of his crew members told him that his tools were gone. The locked hallway closet door had been broken open. As Hal listened to his work crew explain the problem, he looked around. He saw a neighbor standing idly in a front yard across the street watching their activity. According to Hal's work crew, that neighbor had been watching them work all week.

Hal called to this neighbor and motioned him over. As the man walked over, Hal pulled his wallet from his pocket. He opened it and, as his neighbor watched, he pulled out a concealed carry permit, which allows him to carry a gun. He asked the neighbor if he knew what it was, and his neighbor read it aloud. Then Hal asked him about the missing tools. He said that he would eventually find out who took his tools and take care of things.

This neighbor left town that day and didn't return until Hal's work crew finished. He'd received the message loud and clear.

Hal has also learned how to send a message when starting to manage complexes in troubled areas. First, he looks for the local gossip—the one man or woman in the complex who knows about everyone and everything that goes on, then takes time to talk with this person.

Hal tells this gossip that he has taken over management of the complex, then shows his concealed carry permit. He says that he's not going to put up with any crap because, well, something's wrong with him. He doesn't really know why, but sometimes he just loses it. Then he apologizes and says he's sure that nothing will happen.

This method works. When Hal recently took over managing an 18-unit building, he talked to the local gossip right away. Miraculously, within one month, three known troublemakers had moved out.

89. CALL IN THE AUTHORITIES

Seek help from the authorities when you need to evict tenants
whom you suspect are dangerous.

■ ■ ■

Sam Smith (a pseudonym) knew that his deal looked great on
paper, but he didn't realize that his purchase would make headlines in
the newspapers and on radio and television. Here's what happened.

Sam and many other bidders went to the first auction for a house,
but the auctioneer failed to show. The next week, he got lucky. When
the auctioneer showed up and auctioned the house, Sam and one
other man were the only bidders. He won the auction with a $14,000
bid, plus he had to pay off a $14,000 IRS tax lien on the house. Even
$28,000 seemed reasonable, because he estimated that he could rehab
it for $20,000 and sell it for $140,000.

Days after Sam mailed the check to an office in Memphis, he received a courtesy call from someone in that office. That person told
him to be careful, because the previous owner was a militiaman and
had been very difficult to deal with.

Sam had read about cases in which militiamen harassed unsym-
pathetic judges by filing hundreds of liens against their property. They
wanted to use the legal system against them and, by all accounts,
they succeeded. So, when Sam received his deed, he filed it anonymously through a recognized corporate entity. He certainly didn't
want angry militiamen interfering with any of his properties. Then,
after he filed his deed, he filed eviction proceedings against the militiaman living there. When the militiaman didn't make a court appearance or otherwise defend himself, the judge gave Sam a dispossessory
order and wished him good luck.

Armed with his dispossessory order, Sam called the sheriff's department and got the low-down on this militiaman. The sheriff's

department knew him well because his neighbors had filed countless complaints, alleging that he had poisoned their pets and had frequently fired weapons in his backyard. According to the neighbors, he was a master marksman who was able to draw a pistol and shoot moving squirrels in distant trees.

When Sam gave the sheriff's department his dispossessory order, the department made calls to the city and state police departments; the state bureau of investigation; the Bureau of Alcohol, Tobacco, and Firearms (ATF); and the FBI. The sheriff's department took a SWAT team and a fleet of 40 Ford Crown Victorias to serve the dispossessory papers.

The militiaman had seen them coming, so—as they watched—he stationed weapons at every window and door. Then he came outside wearing a bulletproof vest wrapped in explosives, pointed a machine gun in their direction, and held up his child. This event occurred after the Branch Davidian standoff at Waco, so state and federal figures were quite concerned.

After consulting among themselves, the authorities decided to leave. The militiaman apparently thought that he'd won a great battle. Within days, the FBI set up surveillance in a half-vacant duplex across the street from Sam's occupied house. After a few weeks of constant surveillance, the FBI decided that it knew the militiaman's routines well enough to act. So one day, when he left the house and drove down the street, state and federal forces swarmed in and arrested him.

Sam had previously snapped one quick photo—for house insurance purposes. Otherwise, he had avoided taking photos or staring longingly at the house, because he suspected the militiaman dealt harshly with "spies." Now, with him in jail, Sam could finally look over his newly acquired house. In the front yard of the fenced compound were six hungry German Shepherds, and the militiaman's national flag flew from the flagpole. (Sam recognized it because an officer had pointed out the same flag on a plate on the front bumper of the militiaman's car.)

Still, Sam couldn't enter his house for a couple of days after the militiaman departed. ATF officers and bomb squads had to clear each room one at a time. And for the next few days, they realized how completely the militiaman had fulfilled the reason for putting the *F* (for firearms) into the name ATF. News accounts quoted an ATF official as saying that anyone within ten miles of the house certainly had reason to be afraid.

Although his mental state could be questioned, the militiaman's talents as a machinist were apparently second to none. For many years, he had made a living making and selling custom weapons to militia groups across America and around the world. In the mid-1990s, he had even sold weapons to al-Qaida.

Apparently this militiaman had been preparing for Y2K, because they found food, water, and other survival materials in his basement. He had also stockpiled dozens of fully automatic weapons, pipe bombs, hand grenades, antitank weapons, and more than one million rounds of ammunition. As a result, he was charged with numerous counts of federal weapons violations and was eventually sentenced to ten years in prison for each count. He was also charged with several federal and state tax law violations.

As it turned out, the militiaman had plenty of money for his defense. The ATF tore out a false wall and hired a welder to open a safe hidden behind it. Inside, they found several dozen boxes of gold Krugerrands. In court, his defenses were, first, that he was his own sovereign not subject to the laws of the United States of America and, second, that—as a foreigner being held against his will—he was a prisoner of war. For that reason, he later wrote letters to Queen Elizabeth II and Pope John Paul II asking for their intercession on his behalf and seeking to form political alliances with them.

As for Sam, he's grateful that someone tipped him off and that he got the authorities involved to deal with this dangerous situation. He advises others to do the same.

■ TIPS

67. Check laws and regulations before you start land development, plus check them as the job continues because they can change at any time. Also, be prepared for any government-related approvals to take four times longer than you planned for!

68. Sellers aren't always the kind of people they appear to be.

69. To make sure that the house you want to buy is physically located on the land that you're buying, order a survey and title search before you make a purchase.

70. Trust your intuition or gut feeling and things will usually work out better.

71. Draw your neighbors into your building plans and ask for their support on any variance issues.

72. Insure your properties with policies that will cover all contingencies, including lost income.

73. Maintain liability insurance to cover property owners and managers because tenants can sue for the strangest reasons.

74. If you're an investor who builds houses, know what your insurance covers and be sure to purchase Completed Operations insurance.

75. Be sure to order professional property inspections before closing on a property.

76. "Vacant" and "abandoned" houses aren't always found to be as advertised. Use caution when entering them and don't go in by yourself.

77. Don't let long-term renters limit prospective buyers' ability to view your property.

78. Be prepared to defend your actions—in court if necessary.

79. Know how to identify the investment home you purchased at auction to avoid having to break into it.

80. Always research title issues and buy title insurance to cover any surprises.

81. Keep your moral scruples about you when dealing with tenants.

82. What looks good on the outside could be a cesspool on the inside.

83. As a long-distance landlord, even if you rely on trusted agents and managers, still do your own market research.

84. Walk into foreclosure situations with your eyes open and the sheriff's department at your side, if necessary.

85. Take off your rose-colored glasses when doing your due diligence.

86. Always buy title insurance—even for your flips!

87. If you want a title search done right, do it yourself or hire a title company you trust to do it correctly.

88. Reduce your theft troubles by not doing certain things and not saying other things.

89. Seek help from the authorities when you need to evict tenants you suspect are dangerous.

PART 5

LESSONS IN REHABILITATION

■ ■ ■

You finally found a great piece of real estate, and it looks like a strong deal. The selected property has been on the market for a long time, the listing is about to expire, and the owner seems desperate to sell. You just have to name your price and it's yours.

That's not as easy as it sounds.

First, you need to know what you'll have to do to fix up, or rehab, the property. Your first consideration is who will be using it. (If the inhabitants are human, that's a start.) You know you need to comply with human sanitation, fire, and other humane requirements. Once you meet the legal requirements for rehabbing a property, though, every other component to consider is up for grabs in terms of ideals and costs.

All successful real estate investors eventually realize that everyone has their own picture of an ideal home. When you look for the home you're going to live in, you look for your own ideal picture. When you help others find their own homes, you look for their ideal picture. You may already own their ideal picture of a home in the form of a rental house or apartment, trailer or vacation home, single room or warehouse. Forget your prejudices and your own preconceived picture of the ideal home and help someone else find theirs.

Next, once you've determined what you want to do to rehab the property, decide who can do the work for you. Legally, you may need to hire a licensed contractor to do the job. If you don't get one and get caught breaking some codes, it could cost you a lot of money. Whichever route you take, you will have a variety of rehab expenses to guess at. Then, once you know what those expenses will be, you can work on your budget and, from there, finalize the deal.

You'll see from the following stories that investors take a variety of approaches to rehabbing properties into picture-perfect homes.

90. TO REPAIR OR NOT TO REPAIR

Is it better to fix something or replace it? That is the question!

■ ■ ■

Calvin Keeton is likely not alone in agonizing over what an investor should repair instead of replace when getting a property ready for sale or lease.

He hit a low point when he stood in the junk store after dusk using only a clip-on flashlight to sift through a rusty file box. He was searching for an appliance switch that might prove to be obsolete. While scavenging through the dark box, Calvin kept asking himself, "Why am I down at an old warehouse on Main Street searching in the dark for one little thing?" While kicking himself verbally, he reminded himself, "Because I made it my mission to salvage that stove, and now I have to find the right switch to repair it."

Calvin also kept telling himself that, while he knew of easier ways to find and buy a replacement stove, he could get a replacement part cheaper at this junk store—at least sometimes. But this time, he had to confess, "It just wasn't worth it."

91. YOUR FIRST FIXER-UPPER IS THE WORST

Rehabbing your first fixer-upper takes much longer than
expected and costs much more, but it provides you
with a tremendous learning experience.

■ ■ ■

In April 2003, Renée Margaret bought a 1920s cottage in a low-income neighborhood of Nashville, Tennessee, for $28,000. "This was a great deal for my first fixer-upper . . . or so I thought." she says.

Her plan was to take three months to rehab the house. She'd finish in late July and sell it by September so she could go on a long-overdue vacation.

The reality didn't quite match her plan. She tells how the best of plans can go awry when it comes to rehabbing a house.

"After being delayed a week and a half because of rain in May, the framer finally made it out and framed in an exterior porch to be converted into a master bath. Fortunately, the framer and his Spanish-speaking crew worked in a timely manner. When the framer left for another project, the crew proceeded quickly with the work despite my lack of being able to speak Spanish with them. At the time I thought, 'This is a great beginning. So far, so good.'

"Then I made my first mistake of many: I used only one handyman for demolition instead of a crew. He had to demolish the existing bathroom, the kitchen ceiling, the enclosure around the basement steps, and twin closets. All this took a while—at $25 an hour. I was already over budget on this, but I figured I could make it up by hiring quality subs going forward.

"Next, I hired a plumber, and the plumber's assistant did the rough in. We had a small misunderstanding about the placement of the pipes for the bathroom sink, so I called the plumber who insisted the pipes had been put exactly where I said. After a heated discussion, I met the plumber and his assistant at the house early one morning to go over this issue. The plumber wanted to charge me $50 an hour to adjust this minor problem.

"Well, weighing the pros and cons of the entire project, I decided to get this part over with and proceed. So the plumber's assistant came back and placed the pipes the way they were supposed to be done the first time. Then I fired the plumber and he responded by threatening to put a lien on the property. After this mishap—and after I found out that he'd threatened the HVAC man, which I called him on—I have not seen this plumber again.

"Next, we needed to put in a 2.5-ton central heat and air unit. The HVAC man was in the middle of another house-from-hell scenario that month, so he came back and forth to my fixer-upper when he could. It turned out it took a few weeks just for the rough in.

"Next comes putting in the electricity. My house inspector recommended the electrician I hired. He had also warned me about the intelligence level of many subcontractors. Well, this pronouncement made itself clear the day the electrician was supposed to do the rough in—he never showed.

"I called his cell phone for five days and eventually was able to get through to leave a message. When I finally spoke to him, he told me his car had broken down, his girlfriend had kicked him out, and he had no money for transportation or to buy materials for the rough in. I told him I'd pick him up and buy the materials. Even that offer didn't motivate him, because I never heard from him again.

"My search began again for an electrician whose estimate would be close to the no-show electrician's quote. After meeting with nine other electricians over six weeks, I finally found one whose estimate fell within my limited budget. Well, when this guy came out to give me a bid, he had the lovely aroma of pot on him. He slurred his speech and spaced out quite a bit while we talked. 'Great,' I thought, 'This is what I'm reduced to? Hiring a hippie masquerading as a licensed electrician?' Still, with the rehab at a complete standstill for six weeks waiting on an electrician, I did hire him.

"Given that he charged by the hour, which I didn't want to pay (I wanted to pay by the estimate so this would be one less person I'd have to baby-sit by the hour), he showed up at 10:10 AM, only ten minutes late. 'Good. Maybe this fellow will be all right, pot and all,' I thought.

"The first day went well. The second day, he said he'd arrive at 9:00 AM, so I got there just before 9:00 AM. No electrician. I called him at 9:30 AM, and he said, 'I'll get the work done that I said I would.' But it wasn't until 11:30 AM that he finally pulled up. I had some firm but professional words to say like, 'Call if you're going to be late.' To that he replied, '**** this. You're not my employer.' I said, 'It's basic courtesy to call.' He looked perplexed for a while (or maybe he was stoned), and as I walked away, he shouted, 'Hey, no hard feelings!' To make up for it, he said he'd work until 7 PM. ('Great. I'll have to stay until then to baby-sit him!') Then, at 4:30 PM, he said he had a stomachache and had to go home. Before I could say 'What?!' he drove off and shouted that he'd be back at 9:00 the next morning.

"This sounded too familiar. Given that the humidity of a southern summer was in full swing and sweating came easily over this project, I sure didn't need a daily incident like this. Especially when, the following day, he was again a few hours late. I was steaming but decided to focus on the drywall crew that showed up unannounced, ironically just after the drywall was delivered.

"The drywall crew stumbled out of a truck and, amidst an incredible amount of shouting back and forth, energetically started drywalling the front rooms. Meanwhile, I was concerned that the weight of the drywall would bring the house down, not to mention the weight of seven men bustling about inside, too. Well, at this point, my mind was spinning, and as drywall was flying everywhere and landing in the nearly full dumpster, I realized that I had underestimated the extent of my dumpster use.

"Over the next few weeks, the handyman completely demolished the kitchen ceiling, the former enclosure to the basement stairs, the existing bathroom, and the twin closets. He had also framed in a new single closet, a hallway, and another closet. And he'd cut out a 36-inch doorway from the living room into the kitchen. In the process, the floor plan had to be altered.

"Meanwhile, in the evenings, I realized I had to clean up after the drywall crew, because I was going to paint the entire interior myself. This was not in the original plans. The painter, who said he could skim the cracks on the plaster walls, had changed his mind about doing this, so I decided to have the entire house drywalled. That meant my budget for interior painting went out the window and I had to become the painter.

"Being the painter also meant that in the evening, I cleaned up the drywall in the two front rooms so I could begin to paint. Little did I realize how time-consuming it would be to clean drywall dust off the ceilings, walls, and closets. I needed a sturdy straw broom, facemasks, long-sleeved shirts, gloves, a radio to pass the time, and gallons of drinking water to stay cool. Did I mention that the air conditioning wasn't working yet and it was summer in Nashville?

"By this time, the rough-ins for electric and plumbing had passed inspection, although the central heat and air had not. It seems that the codes inspector had five minor issues with some things, and the HVAC man had his own issues with codes. Eventually, the HVAC man rough-in passed inspection, the majority of the drywall was up, the electrician from the hippie era started the trim out, and I found a new plumber.

"Meanwhile, the handyman was doing a meticulous job on everything, which I told him he didn't have to. After all, I was paying him $25 an hour. He liked this; I didn't. He had his standards; I had my budget. I pushed him daily to pick up the pace of his work and made numerous trips to Home Depot and Lowe's for him.

"Renovations progressed slowly but surely. I hired a painter to start painting the exterior, only to discover the paint was a different shade of sage green in every gallon of paint we had. Plus he was only able to work half days because of the incredible heat and humidity.

"Meanwhile, the head of the shrub removal crew wanted to get paid, although he hadn't yet finished the job, so my withholding his pay provided instant motivation for him to complete it the day he said he would, even if he did wait until 7 PM that day to finish. I went home for the evening, only to get a phone call to come back because, he said, he'd now finished the job. When I got there, he hadn't finished, so I waited until he did.

"Next, the building inspector informed me that the vaulted kitchen ceiling and all the new walls needed insulation. 'How hard can that be? I'll do it myself,' I thought, eager to save some money. (I had forgotten to add insulation into the budget.) I was told that installing insulation in each bathroom should take about two hours—but it took me seven hours for just one bathroom. After a few evenings, I managed to complete insulating the bathrooms and started on the kitchen ceiling and the kitchen's knee walls. After putting in many hours, I hired a contractor to finish the job. However, the morning he was supposed to show, I got a call that he was in the hospital. Meanwhile, I had already called the building inspector to come back and approve the insulation. Oops on that timing!

"Before long, the insulation on the kitchen ceiling got finished, the inspector passed all the rough-ins, and my attention turned to finishing the remaining drywall in the back rooms. The drywall crew arrived again the way it did the first time: unannounced and full of vigor and noise. When the drywall was 90 percent complete, Roberto, the head hombre, decided to leave a few walls undone. Once again, I found that withholding pay worked wonders. His crew finished everything except for one closet; the handyman finished that part of the job.

"With all the drywall up, the trim-outs for electric and HVAC man could begin. Again, the electrician arrived when it suited him, and the HVAC man continued to have issues with the codes inspector, who was going to pull all of his permits. I wasn't sure who was at fault and was ready to sue both of them, but mostly I wanted to get the central heating and air completed so the house could get air conditioning. After all, it was August by this time! After making a phone call to the HVAC man (against whom I threatened legal action if he didn't finish the job), he got it done quickly.

"The electrician had wrapped up, so I started delivering the kitchen cabinets a few at a time in the back of my station wagon. After the handyman installed these cabinets, I sanded, stained, and polyurethaned them. At that point, I could finally say the house was coming together and it looked great. The only major work left was the trim-out for plumbing (no problems), finishing the hardwood floors (great), putting a final coat of paint on the trim work (my job), painting the front porch and landscaping (me), trash duty (me), and cleaning the interior and washing the windows (me).

"Throughout the project, a few junkies and/or drug dealers passed by the house, and neighbors shouted comments about this project from across the street—when they weren't yelling at each other.

"Three months after I'd planned for the house to be finished with its rehab, it finally was. By then it was October 2003. I put the house on the market in November, advertised it in local papers, and put up a For Sale by Owner sign. I reasoned that, because I went over budget by $8,000, I would save by not paying commissions and make a profit by selling it myself.

"However, selling a house in a low-income neighborhood during the holidays—and competing with the Titans and Vanderbilt football games—became the final challenge. I held seven open houses on four Sundays in November and three in December. I received 78 phone calls but no offers because the neighborhood didn't have a lot of appeal. My holding costs mounted, so I put the house on the market with a real estate agent in March 2004. I got a full-price offer quickly from an out-of-state buyer. His offer was $84,900, but he wanted $2,500 toward closing, $500 toward repairs, $500 toward appliances, and a home warranty policy costing $409. After getting advice to go ahead with the sale, I accepted the offer and got out from under this fixer-upper. The closing was in April—seven months later than I had planned.

"No, I didn't make a profit on my first fixer-upper. Therefore, I had to spend my vacation relaxing on my back porch after sunset and anticipating buying my next dandy of a fixer-upper."

92. OWNING REHABS ISN'T ALWAYS ROSES

Beware of falling into the rehab trap.

■ ■ ■

Have you ever caught the bug that sets you up with these enticing words: "Fabulous wealth can be yours if you buy junkers and turn them into palaces."

David Finkel (http://www.resultsnow.com) learned that millions can be made in rehab projects, but he advises doing a lot of soul searching before diving into this type of investing. It's simply not right for everyone.

He says, "I've discovered that rehabs aren't for me. In my opinion, they all too often take too much money up front, too much energy to complete, and too much time to turn when selling them. The first causes you to have too much risk. The second cuts in on your efforts to find more deals. And the third eats into your margins and cash flow. Rehabs turn many an investor into a motivated seller."

David's rule of thumb is that if a house needs more than minor cosmetic work, then flip the deal to another party.

93. NOVICE INVESTORS' REHAB MISTAKES

If you waste time getting work completed on your rehabs,
you're wasting your profit.

■ ■ ■

Some novice investors called Miami investor Pat Kiehl, asking for advice. They were having difficulty selling a rehab house and asked Pat to take a look and offer suggestions.

The first thing that Pat noticed when he drove up to the property was that the lawn needed to be cut. (Remember, every house only gets one chance to make a first impression.) Added to that was the fact that the yard provided no place to park. So Pat's first suggestion was to make a parking space from landscape timbers and add a few stepping stones to the doorway. He said, "You can put down mulch or gravel (depending on code) for the parking area, then plant some flowers around to add a nice touch. Paint the exterior of the house an attractive color, too."

The house's entrance opened into a large family room that appeared very plain. Pat suggested putting up wallpaper borders to break up the monotony of the walls and add a small table or two with a plant or other décor items that are inexpensive yet attractive. "Even bring some of these things from your own home," he suggested.

Walking through the house, Pat noticed lots of little things that weren't completed—plus materials stacked in various areas, dust here and there, and so on. Knowing that the novice investors had owned the property for six months, he asked why the rehabbing wasn't completely finished. "Well," he was told, "the handyman didn't work out and had to be terminated." Though the owners knew they had to finish it off, they were also working full-time. Looking back, they confessed, they chose that particular handyman because his estimate was a few hundred dollars less than other quotes they received from faster, more reliable contractors. Besides, the owners hadn't considered the expense of four or five additional monthly mortgage payments when deciding to hire an unproven person at a lower cost. In the long run, what really would have been cheaper?

Pat asked about marketing the house and learned that they had held open houses already. "With the house in this condition, no wonder no one was interested," he commented. To make it more marketable, he gave them the following suggestions.

Complete rehabbing the house right away. Get the fans up, wall plates installed, floors cleaned, and carpets installed. (It had no carpeting yet!) Hide unused materials in a closet. Certainly don't leave them in the open where prospective buyers could see them.

Disperse attractive décor items in the family room (the first room to be seen), the kitchen, and the bathrooms. Even burn some cinnamon incense during the open house to make the whole house smell nice.

Because the property spans two lots, place two signs in the yard and put reflective numbers on them so the contact phone numbers can be seen more easily than if they'd been written with magic markers. Attach information tubes with descriptive fliers. Also, tape one flier to the inside of the window in case the fliers in the box run out.

Cut the grass, plant a few flowers, build a driveway, and in general make the front yard look more appealing.

Price the house accordingly. Don't keep raising the price just because it takes longer to sell it, and if you do raise the price, make sure the house looks better than any of the other houses around. It should be shown in *pristine* condition.

Pat says it's a good idea for investors to rehab the first one or two houses themselves to get an idea how long it should take for certain jobs. However, if it's not possible to work on it full-time, it will be cheaper in the long run to hire a handyman to work on it full-time, reducing the months it sits empty without bringing in rent.

94. IS THE RIGHT WORK GETTING DONE?

Make sure the independent contractors you hire are doing
their work properly.

■ ■ ■

For many years, Ginny Pitts and her partners at Grand Canyon Properties in Nashville, Tennessee, hired the services of an experienced, 80-year-old man who had a business mowing lawns. Whenever a Grand Canyon property required mowing, they simply called the Lawnmower Man and gave him the proper address. The Lawn-mower Man would mow the lawn and drop off an invoice at the office a few days later.

One day, the Lawnmower Man called the office to ask about a job on Argyle Avenue—a vacant rehab he'd already been mowing for several weeks. He wanted to know, specifically, what to do about the padlock and chain on the backyard fence. "Well," Ginny thought, "that seems to explain the notice to abate nuisance due to tall grass that they had just received." She instructed him, "Go ahead and cut the padlock and chain so you can mow the backyard."

Then the Lawnmower Man replied, "Okay—but won't the man with the boat mind?"

"What man?"

"The one with the boat," the Lawnmower Man repeated.

"What boat?"

"The one in the backyard with the fence around it."

Ginny immediately declared, "But this is a vacant house. There's no boat in the backyard."

"No, someone lives there," the Lawnmower Man responded.

Startled, Ginny wondered, "Has someone moved into our house and brought a boat into the yard?" After a few more minutes of questioning, Ginny realized that the Lawnmower Man had been mowing the *wrong* yard all this time. He'd been mowing the front yard at 1105 Argle Avenue instead of 1105 Argyle Avenue, and the people on Argle had been receiving lawnmower service at Ginny's expense!

95. TURNING A LEMON INTO LEMONADE

A lemon of a zoning conflict was turned into lemonade and
put $50,000 into the investor's pocket.

■ ■ ■

A few years ago, Jeff Gaw purchased a property in Sylvan Park, an up-and-coming area of Nashville, Tennessee. The property was an old house that had been converted into a fiveplex by a previous owner some 30 years before. This fiveplex was fully rented and needed very little rehab work, so Jeff felt justified in believing that the asking price of $185,000 made it an excellent deal. But before he actually closed on it, he checked the rent rolls and discovered that one of the tenants was the seller's nephew. His research told him the nephew was under treatment for schizophrenia and, from all records and reports, seemed to be okay as a tenant. Jeff went ahead and closed the transaction.

Within a few months after Jeff closed the deal, he received a call from the nephew. Surprised that Jeff had bought the property, the nephew complained that he was supposed to have inherited the property and it wasn't right for Jeff to own it. Apparently, he had also complained to his family members. When no one seemed to care, the nephew contacted the city codes department to get Jeff in trouble. As it turns out, he succeeded.

Jeff had done his homework but not thoroughly. Before closing, Jeff had inspected the applicable zoning regulations and noticed that the property was still zoned as a single-family residence. Jeff assumed that the house was grandfathered in before the zoning ordinance had taken effect. As it turned out, the owner who converted the property had never applied for the permit that would have grandfathered his conversion. That meant Jeff was operating the fiveplex in contravention of zoning regulations. City codes gave him 30 days to cure it (that is, return the property to a single family residence). Jeff knew that would be physically impossible, so he contacted his lawyer, who was able to get some extensions.

Thankfully, Jeff had some experience in rehabs and conversions. Because he knew homes in the area were appreciating quickly, Jeff decided to do the conversion in a first-class way. He totally gutted the house and rebuilt the 2,900-square-foot interior with fine amenities. It took a year to do the conversion, but it was worth it. He sold the house for a near-record-setting amount of $400,000, making a $50,000 profit. Since then, other homes in the area have sold for more than that, but Jeff's converted house is still considered one of the finest and has even been featured on a local Nashville homes tour television program. He certainly turned a lemon into lemonade!

96. THE VALUE OF A SKILLED, STEADY HANDYMAN

Do everything within your power to keep a good handyman
working for you if you find an honest and skilled one.

■ ■ ■

In the four years that Craig Schiesser has been investing, he has dealt with a lot of handymen. Handymen, of course, charge less than contractors and often get to a job faster, but some are untrustworthy, dishonest, and not very skilled. Then there's the additional problem of taxation and liability issues.

Contractors are insured so the investor is not liable for their work or their workers. By contrast, if a handyman or his or her workers become injured on a job, the investor may be held liable. In addition, if an investor pays a handyman more than $700 in a year, this has to be reported to the IRS; because contractors are separate business entities, the investor doesn't need to make such a report.

Craig appreciates having found a good handyman to make repairs on his investment properties. As he says, "I'm very happy that what I do is benefiting someone else, and his work is benefiting me. Having this asset has, in fact, driven some of the investment decisions that I have made.

"When I started investing, I hired one handyman for a very small job, a minor outdoor electrical job. When this guy showed up, he brought a friend, and between them and their drinking, it took them 8 hours to do 90 minutes worth of work. I never called them back. In another situation, the handyman just didn't show up. Because these were small jobs, I wasn't out much. That's the price you pay to learn."

About three unsuccessful handymen later, he found a really honest one—an ex-con, about 50 years old, who had been free for more than 15 years. Not only did he do well on his first small job, but he advised Craig on how to do it better and cheaper. Craig says, "I learned more about him. He goes to church faithfully two or three times a week. He even drives a church bus and works on a telephone hotline."

Since the first job this handyman did, he has made repairs to two other properties and completely rehabbed three single-family houses and a duplex, including some full gutting jobs. "Early on, I used to tell him what I wanted, but now we confer and I've learned to defer to his ideas. Not only does he save me money, but he has taught me a lot. I pay him every two weeks when he's doing a job.

"When a project is completed, we sit down for a nice dinner and finalize the deal. I usually pay him more than he asks because of how much I appreciate his work."

On large jobs, Craig still hires licensed contractors for some things his handyman cannot or will not do—such as servicing forced-air furnaces, for example. Craig says, "It would likely be faster to hire a lot of different contractors to do various activities, but it would cost more money than using my good handyman.

"I'm not shy to tell him that I'm making money from his labors. He, too, acknowledges that he's making money, and since we've been working together, his yearly income has doubled." But this investor believes that the best part of the relationship is sharing skills and enjoying the experience of working with "this honest and honorable person."

■ TIPS

90. Is it better to fix something or replace it? That is the question!

91. Rehabbing your first fixer-upper takes much longer than expected and costs much more, but it provides you with a tremendous learning experience.

92. Beware of falling into the "rehab" trap.

93. If you waste time getting work completed on your rehabs, you're wasting your profit.

94. Make sure independent contractors you hire are doing their work properly.

95. A lemon of a zoning conflict was turned into lemonade and put $50,000 into the investor's pocket.

96. Do everything within your power to keep a good handyman working for you if you find an honest and skilled one.

PART 6

YOUR ROLE
AS AN INVESTOR

. . .

You've seen infomercials and e-mails featuring real estate millionaires and "get rich quick" deals. Now you've decided that it's your turn to get rich.

Yes, you know that you're going to be a millionaire—once you really start hitting home runs investing in real estate. You can hardly wait for the day when you can quit your full-time job and lead a life of relaxation and luxury like a retired major league player. Just like you, most successful real estate investors started investing in real estate because they wanted to improve their lifestyles.

One of the first things that all successful real estate investors realize is that their role is to be businesspeople running an investment company. That means that if you want to be a successful real estate investor, you must be a successful business manager. Start by writing down a long-term business plan and goals that you can reach. Learn as much as possible from other real estate professionals. Get adequate insurance coverage for the unexpected and the inexplicable. Keep organized records, because the tax collector could come take away your profits if your bookkeeping isn't handled right.

All real estate investors, including you, play a variety of important roles in our society. If you're a landlord, you help provide housing for approximately one-third of all Americans. If you are a rehabber, your activities are the essence of many urban renewal projects. If you're a hard moneylender, you provide the grease that keeps the investing machine going. If you are a real estate investment guru, you provide the inspiration and guidance on which many investors rely. If you help more of your fellow investors than you hurt, you have done well in your role as real estate investor. Congratulations. You're part of an essential team.

Now do as the following storytellers have done—get out there and play ball.

97. INVESTING IN REAL ESTATE VERSUS STOCKS

Any investment that you can add value to, realize tax benefits
from, and actually see and touch should be a good one.

■ ■ ■

Charles Benn had just started investing in the stock market in
late November 2002. He invested $2,000 in various stocks through
online trading. He recalls, "I watched them go down, as always, just
after I brought them. I made my money back on other stocks early
the next year. But then I discovered real estate, which I found was a
much better investment than stocks for me."

Why? The big reason is that he could get others to lend him the
money he needed to invest. That loan could be anywhere from 70 to
100 percent loan-to-value of the property. He says, "I found that I
could buy a house, rent it out, have someone else pay down the loan
for me, and that still allowed me to make money. That, combined with
depreciation, meant that I would pay very little in taxes for the money
I made from renting the property. If I made any improvements, I could
deduct them or depreciate them, which meant I would pay even less
in taxes.

"Real estate investing is one of those businesses in which the
government really works with you to help you increase your wealth.
That's not true for people who invest in the stock market."

Another reason he prefers real estate over the stocks is that, "I
don't have to worry about an Enron problem happening with the
property I own." Because the real estate market moves a lot more
slowly than the stock market, he won't see his profits disappear in a
day as can happen with stocks. "Plus, with real estate, if there is a
problem overseas, my house value is not going to drop. If it does
drop, it would be a gradual decrease, not a roller coaster ride down-
hill. I can control the value of my investments to a large degree, and

I can repair certain items around the house to increase its overall value. When I owned stocks, there was really nothing I could do to increase my investment value."

On a final note, he says that if he runs into hard times, he can always move into his investment properties. "I could never move into anything I owned in the stock market," he quips.

98. LOOKING BACK WITH SOME REGRET

It's never too late to start becoming a real estate investor.

■ ■ ■

Jeanne Hoechst-Ronner had always wanted to own real estate, but her husband was reluctant to risk even buying a home, so she did nothing.

Eight years ago, Jeanne's status changed. She became a divorced mother and joined the Real Estate Investors of Nashville (REIN). Unfortunately, despite the education and support she received from REIN, she still hesitated to take the first step and buy a property. After all, she had two children, more bills to pay, and less disposable income to cover her expenses.

However, six months ago, Jeanne took that first step and started investing in real estate. Today, her biggest regret is that she didn't buy a property eight years ago, especially because she's seen houses in her neighborhood increase in value by at least 133 percent. And, inspired by Jeanne's excitement, her ex-husband has recently purchased his fourth investment property.

It's never too late—at least for investing in real estate.

99. FLEXIBILITY AND CREATIVITY PAY OFF

Finding creative ways to lease properties puts more money
in your pocket.

■ ■ ■

John Thomas (a pseudonym) owns a condominium in one of
Nashville's affluent neighborhoods. For many years, he advertised the
unit for lease in a conventional manner in papers and on street signs.
At the time, he was renting the condominium for $600 a month.

Several years ago, he received a call from someone in the human
resources department of a record company operating in Nashville.
The HR specialist asked him if he would lease the condominium to
the record company. When John asked about the terms they wanted,
he was told that personnel from New York and Los Angeles occasionally stayed in extended-stay suites in Nashville for three to four
weeks at a time. The record company would like to lease the condominium on a long-term basis, but the actual occupants would change
regularly.

Agreeable to the idea, John still needed to determine the rate. He
guessed that the record company was paying at least $50 a day for
the extended-stay suites, so he decided to charge $50 a day for the
monthly average of 30 days. He said he would charge $1,500 a
month if they rented monthly, $1,450 a month if they rented quar-
terly, $1,400 a month if they rented semiannually, or $1,350 a month
if they rented annually. John had correctly concluded that the record
company would pay a premium so the occupants would have more
of a "home" and less of a "hotel room."

That record company leased John's condominium for three annual terms. When it stopped leasing the property, he contacted human
resource departments at other record companies and quickly found

another one willing to lease his condominium under equally profitable terms.

100. APPEARANCE AFFECTS HOW PEOPLE PERCEIVE YOU

You never really know what impression you are making
on a prospective seller.

■ ■ ■

Smart landlords don't drive their fanciest cars or wear their nicest clothes when they visit their properties. We live in a litigious society, and people with "deep pockets" make easy targets, so smart landlords don't want their tenants to see them looking rich. Experienced Nashville landlord Hal Wilson drives an older sport utility vehicle and dresses modestly. But even Hal doesn't always realize the impression his appearance makes on others.

Several years ago, while "driving for dollars," Hal discovered what he thought was a vacant house. In addition to noticing high grass in the yard, he saw no car in the driveway, no lights on inside, and no visible movement in or around the house. He called the courthouse and found the name and address of the woman who owned the "vacant" house.

As it turned out, the owner worked near the vacant house but she lived on the other side of town. She allowed a relative to live there free, so it was occupied; the resident just kept strange hours. However, the owner said she was interested in selling. She was, in fact, being wooed by five other active investors in town. So, Hal repeatedly met her at her place of work, took her out for treats, and even drove her home a few times after their meetings.

Finally one day, she called and told Hal that she wanted to sell the house to him. He thanked her profusely and started the paperwork. Soon after, he received a call from another investor, a competitor for buying this house. His competitor complained that the owner had previously promised him the house, so he'd called to ask why she was now selling it to Hal. She had told the competitor that she felt sorry for Hal because he wasn't very well off.

How did she come to that conclusion? During one of their visits at her work place, they sat down to drink coffee and Hal crossed one leg over the other. Poor Hal says that he hadn't noticed the hole in his shoe, but she certainly had and drew her own conclusions.

Well, Hal spent a lot of money rehabbing her house, but in the end, he made a $40,000 profit. Now he can afford to fix the hole in his shoe!

101. KNOWING ENOUGH

You'll never know it all, but you can learn *enough*.

■ ■ ■

David Finkel is coauthor of *Making Big Money Investing in Foreclosures* (http://www.resultsnow.com). He says, "When I first started investing, I kept learning more and more but never felt like I knew enough. Then one day, I realized the key: people know enough when they step out and take action, understanding that they'll never know it all.

"I believe this leap of faith is the final ingredient of success."

102. SELECT A TEAM TO SUPPORT YOUR STYLE

Build a power team of professionals who understand your
investment goals and style.

■ ■ ■

In September 2003, Sergeant First Class Kristopher Bender left
the Army to invest in real estate full-time. Kris admits that, in their
younger years, he and his wife Michelle were financially irresponsi-
ble. As Michelle developed an interest in Rich Dad's CASHFLOW
101 board game and Kris researched real estate investing, they realized that they needed to become financially responsible. They were
inspired by the financial guidance of Dave Ramsey, a nationally syn-
dicated radio personality and financial self-help guru.

During his first year of full-time investing, Kris kept reading
about the cost-saving and paper-simplifying benefits of simultaneous closings. Simultaneous closings occur when two or more related
purchase and sales transactions occur one after the other, usually in
one closing office at the direction of one closing agent or attorney.
Most often, there is one middle party who is the buyer in the first
transaction and the seller in the second transaction. The aim is for the
middle party to save money and time. The middle party actually does
own the property for the short time that passes between the transactions and is named on the chain of title. (Therefore, it's wise for the
middle party to buy title insurance.)

After reading about simultaneous closings, Kris decided that he
would attempt one. He submitted an offer to buy a fourplex in Clarksville, Tennessee, which the lender had foreclosed on and now owned.
Because the lender was located in Mississippi and likely wanted to
get this distant property off its books, Kris submitted an offer for
$40,000 less than fair market value. He specified in his offer that the
lender pay all closing costs and close at Kris's attorney's office in

Clarksville. The lender accepted Kris's offer on the condition that they close on May 27, or Kris would have to pay $150 a day for delaying the closing.

As soon as Kris accepted this agreement, he advertised the property for sale in the Clarksville newspaper. Within a couple of weeks, he accepted an offer to sell the property on the condition that the buyer pay all his closing costs and also close on May 27. The way Kris had structured the deal, he wouldn't have to pay any closing costs, and he would make a good profit for minimal effort.

But something went wrong.

A few days before the scheduled closing, Kris called his attorney and asked how things were going. His attorney said that he hadn't received any of the closing documents yet, so he couldn't even order a title search. Kris then called the lender and asked how things were going. The lender said that they had already prepared and forwarded the closing documents to the closing attorney. Kris called his attorney again. His attorney, once again, told Kris that he hadn't received any closing documents. When the attorney called the lender directly, he found out that the closing documents had been sent to the *lender's* usual closing attorney, not to Kris's attorney. The lender's attorney didn't ask any questions; he just filed the documents away.

The lender prepared and forwarded another set of closing documents to Kris's attorney, but soon after, the lender told Kris they wouldn't use his attorney after all. All of this communication took a number of days and put them past the May 27 deadline.

For the next three weeks, Kris tried to convince the lender to read the contract and comply with the specified term that they close at *his* attorney's office. Meanwhile, the lender tried to charge Kris $150 for each day of delay that had occurred beyond May 27. Kris finally conducted a conference call with all parties, including the lender, the attorneys, and the real estate agents. Nobody claimed responsibility for the delay, and nobody was willing to pay the $150-a-day fee for delaying the closing. In the end, Kris resorted to his drill sergeant demeanor and dressed down the professionals who were supposed to be helpful. Soon afterward, the lender decided that

Kris shouldn't have to suffer for someone else's mistake and agreed to pay for new documents and drop the late fees, just to get the deal closed. Unfortunately, the delay threw everyone's timing off, and Kris couldn't accomplish a simultaneous closing.

As a result of this closing breaking down, Kris decided that he would only hire—and train, if necessary—top professionals who understood the creative aspects of real estate investing and were willing to help him accomplish his goals.

103. A BIGGER ROLE IN LIFE

When appropriate, take the opportunity to perform a
great service for owners, for neighborhoods, and for families
that need a new direction.

■ ■ ■

One day, investor Jim Greeley received a call from a couple who owned a property in Florida. They had remodeled this house in August to accommodate a new tenant. When it became empty, they decided not to rent the house again because the previous tenant was nothing but trouble. But at the last minute, someone in the neighborhood convinced them to help their niece out of trouble after her life had been threatened by her ex-husband. She and her three children needed a safe haven—preferably close to family. So the owners agreed to let her move in, and her relatives across the street even paid the first month's rent. It was the only rent the owners ever received.

Realizing they'd made a mistake, the owners took a trip to Florida to evict this tenant. Jim met them at the rental house, and what he saw brought him to tears.

The house didn't appear to be in bad condition from the street, although it had a generally unkempt appearance—odd for such a nice neighborhood where houses sold in the low-$100,000s. But Jim knew they faced problems before they walked in because not one, not two, but three different neighbors came out to talk with the owners. They asked in hushed tones, "Have you seen the garage? Pool? Kitchen? You didn't hear it from me, but. . . ."

Looking concerned, they knocked on the door and were greeted by a teenage boy who appeared to be mentally challenged. He shouted for his mother who, yelling from behind a closed door, told them the owners were supposed to arrive that morning. She shouted for them to go away.

But they'd already gotten a glimpse of the disaster inside the house and insisted on being let in. The tenant rushed out while viciously, almost obsessively, brushing her long, filthy hair and shouting every rambling thought imaginable. Then she focused just long enough to say, "Go in then!"

This house, freshly updated only three months before, had been trashed from top to bottom. Not a two-foot stretch of floor was clear of children's clothing. Most of the rooms had no furniture; what little furniture in them was covered by bags of garbage, more children's clothing, broken appliances, newspapers, and animals. The rooms smelled rancid.

They worked their way through the rest of the house, noticing ridiculous amounts of animal feces and urine on the floor in every room. Worse yet, kitchen counters were completely covered—old plates of food with mold and decaying matter, glasses with evaporated liquids of various colors, open boxes of cereal and cat food, pots and pans stacked two feet high, and so much junk in the sink, it was unusable. All of the cabinet doors had been carefully removed— not torn from their hinges, just removed. They still hadn't seen the bathrooms.

As they bucked up the courage to move on, two beautiful little girls about ages two and five ran by them barefoot—barefoot over the rabbit feces and cat urine, over the dirty clothes and stale old food, over the broken plates and into the scarred arms of their mother. This tenant must have been thinking she was about to be evicted from the nicest crack den she'd ever lived in. For Jim, it was disgraceful, disturbing, and compelling all at once.

The bathroom sinks were clogged and the toilets, well, should have been flushed weeks ago. The mirrors were cracked and broken. Every square inch of countertop was covered with debris. Vanity doors were removed (as in the kitchen), and medicine cabinets overflowed with prescription bottles and personal unmentionables.

In the mother's bedroom, several cats lay on the bed. By the smell, it was clear that's where they lived. In this room, so much clothing had been thrown here and there, it was hard to open the door and move around.

At this point, the woman owner broke down and cried, walking out of the house to fall to her knees in tears on the front lawn. Jim and her husband pressed on inside to find the children's rooms with only mattresses on the floor. No sheets, no blankets, no furniture, just mattresses—which, of course, were surrounded by cat litter boxes and still more rabbit feces. In the boy's room, they saw several pairs of brand-new $150 sneakers.

They walked through the family room, where the tenants had destroyed the fireplace, then stepped into the 20-by-20-foot enclosed porch. There, the barnyard smell started to intensify. As the tenant complained at the top of her lungs that the room had no heat or air conditioning, Jim climbed through six-foot mountains of even more discarded clothing, broken furniture, and appliances to get to the once-beautiful enclosed pool. Someone had removed the custom-made wood steps leading down into the area, so they had to jump to the lower level.

Apparently the tenant had trained all of the large-breed dogs in the vicinity to use the sidewalk around the pool as their place to visit after hefty meals. While the rabbit feces and cat urine covered the floors inside the house, dog feces decorated the enclosed pool. It was olfactory overload.

Every inch of wallpaper had been torn off the walls, exposing the drywall. Every light had been smashed or pulled down from the ceiling. The speakers from the stereo system were missing and presumed destroyed. The entire room had once been fitted with a drop ceiling—about eight feet high over the cement walkway surrounding the pool and about 12 feet high over the pool itself. The ceiling had all been ripped down, exposing the underside of the roof.

Jim and the owners reconvened on the front lawn. First and foremost, they recognized the danger those children were in. The food on the floors was either rotten or indistinguishable from pet food. The two-year-old girl probably couldn't tell the difference between Cocoa Puffs and rabbit droppings. The trio couldn't bear the thought of leaving without doing something to protect her and her siblings, so they phoned the police.

In less than ten minutes, an Escambia County sheriff arrived. Unfortunately, in that brief span of time, the mother had recruited the children to clean up as if their lives depended on it. Not only that, she'd changed their clothes from dirty pajamas to unexpectedly clean attire. By the time the owners got back inside, the floors were mostly free of animal and food matter, and the mother was accusing them of telling stories to the police "so they can kick us out at Christmas." She'd clearly been through this scenario before.

Back out on the front lawn, the officer recalled to Jim and the owners how, in the past two months, he'd picked up the mother twice. One night during a heavy storm, he'd found her walking along Gulf Beach Highway without an umbrella. When he pulled over to ask why, her response was, "I need cigarettes, and I'm going to the Winn Dixie." It was well after midnight, and the store was closed. The officer had driven her home.

A month later, he received a 911 call for a "woman down" at a biker bar. Sure enough, she was down all right. Face down in her own vomit. Again, he'd driven her home. Little did he know she had children. Then, just as he finished speaking, another sheriff pulled up. This is where the story really gets bad.

The two beautiful little girls, their faces full of innocence and wonder, panicked. "Mommy, Mommy! Don't let them do it again! Don't let them take us from you! Please, no!" Jim's heart sank, his eyes welling with tears. He had to remind himself that calling the sheriff had nothing to do with how the tenant treated the house. Still, those kids needed rescuing from a mother who preferred putting a glass pipe to her mouth over a forkful of food.

Sadly, the mother and kids had done just enough cleaning that, after an inspection, the second officer judged the house habitable for the children. Barely, but still habitable.

Feeling empowered by that, the mother snatched up the little girls, grabbed her son, and shoved them all inside. "I know my rights!" she shouted. "Now get off my lawn and don't come back unless you have a warrant!"

The officer said she was right and there was nothing else Jim and the owners could do that day.

As an aftermath to this story, Jim wrote, "Have I been through things like this before? More times than I care to remember. But there was such desperation in those little girls' eyes that I couldn't let this one go.

"What did I learn from this? A few things. First, it reinforced the notion that real estate investing is a sincerely noble profession. Looking at the frightened eyes of those owners, I knew I could help them. As their heads spun with confusion and they searched for answers, I was able to guide them toward a solution. I talked to them about the steps needed to evict a tenant properly in Florida and offered to introduce them to a first-rate landlord/tenant attorney who would handle the entire process for them. These solutions helped, but they were still upset about having to deal with a whole new set of problems they hadn't counted on: getting their house ready for sale again.

"Blessed with a good set of skills as a real estate investor, I knew what I could do—and I knew what they needed to hear. I told them if we can get the numbers to work right for both of us, I'll buy the house as-is, for cash. I could see immediate relief in their eyes.

"Real estate investors do make a difference in our communities. By cleaning up the bad elements, we contribute to rising standards and better neighborhoods. In this case, it wouldn't surprise me to receive a few calls of thanks from the neighbors.

"Overall, however, the most important part of this experience is being part of a solution that would help three innocent souls who presently depend on an unstable, negligent parent for everything in their lives. No one knows what will happen for sure, although one way or another, they'll be forced into a new reality soon. Maybe this will be the eviction that shocks the mother so deeply that she turns her life around. Or maybe this will get the kids away from her into a safe household with people who care.

"In situations like this, I tell myself that I'm forcing people up to a higher plane where they can flourish like they didn't know they could before."

Here's a footnote to Jim's story. He says, "In addition to solving problems by putting this deal together, I walked away with $11,000 in my pocket. There's nothing quite like real estate!"

104. CHECK YOUR BELIEFS ABOUT MONEY

Making good money in real estate can cause you to confront deeply hidden beliefs from your past regarding your self-worth and the concept of being rich. These deserve your attention and honest self-evaluation.

■ ■ ■

In David Finkel's (http://www.resultsnow.com) opinion, one of the biggest roadblocks to an investor making a fortune in real estate is having limiting beliefs about self-worth and money. He explains what he went through as a young investor.

"When I started investing, I had trouble selling the properties I picked up. Why? Because on one level or another, I didn't feel good enough about myself to think it was okay to make that much money with so little effort. The concept was alien to me.

"Also, my beliefs about money and what it meant to be rich made 'making money' a dirty thing in my mind. It took several years to clear out this garbage and be comfortable with the wealth that was flowing into my life."

105. SELLERS DON'T REJECT YOU, THEY REJECT OFFERS

Understand that if you never ask, you'll never receive.

■ ■ ■

When David Finkel (http://www.resultsnow.com) first started investing in real estate, he admits feeling scared actually to make an offer to a seller. He says, "The root cause of this was my fear of the seller rejecting me and my offer (for in my mind, the two were the same thing). Over time, I realized that this one mistake kept me from making offers that, in retrospect, I think the seller would have accepted. *Not* realizing this cost me hundreds of thousands of dollars in lost profits.

"Today, I see many other investors falling into this same trap. Sometimes it's guised in the clothing of disbelief that a seller would ever accept a nothing down offer. Sometimes it comes in the form of walking away from a seller with a promise to 'get back to him with an offer' (rather than making the offer on the spot). Beware. The clothing may be different but the cost is still the same.

"The most important lesson I learned from these experiences is that not asking is an automatic no and asking is never as painful as I might have imagined."

106. VALUING A KNOWLEDGEABLE PROPERTY MANAGER

Make your portfolio more profitable by partnering with
a knowledgeable, reliable property manager.

■ ■ ■

When Lyle and Linda Thompson (pseudonyms) relocated to Nashville in 1995, they met Jack Jackson (also a pseudonym), a career real estate investor, real estate broker, and property manager. The Thompsons told Jackson that they wanted to own 10 properties before they both turned 50 in 2001. Jackson assured them that it was very possible. Today, the Thompsons credit Jackson with making that dream come true.

When they moved to Nashville, they knew few people and knew little about real estate values around the city. Jackson helped the Thompsons identify and invest in hot areas of the city. When an older couple who also invested in real estate decided to start liquidating their portfolio, Jackson introduced them to the Thompsons. As a result, they were able to buy a duplex, a fourplex, and an eightplex before the properties even hit the market, and obtain owner financing as well. All three properties were located in the Belmont-Hillsboro area near Music Row and the Vanderbilt and Belmont University communities, considered hot areas. Within the next few years, Jackson also helped the Thompsons buy three more duplexes before they were ever listed. They have certainly profited from their Jackson-guided purchases over the last ten years.

Since 1995, Jackson has also been a close family friend. Although he formally retired from property management two years ago, he still serves the Thompsons as a mentor and personal real estate consultant—a relationship that has been personally and professionally rewarding for everyone. Jackson's example even inspired the Thompsons's youngest son to become a real estate investor, real estate agent, and property manager.

107. TEACH YOUR CHILDREN WELL

Teach your children how to invest early in life.

■ ■ ■

Kerry Baird and her five-year-old daughter, Rebekah, were busy picking weeds in the front yard of a rental property that she and her husband had recently acquired. They had purchased the house to rehab and resell, so they paid special attention to its curb appeal in addition to the interior work it needed.

Kerry started to keep track of the time that her daughter worked on the property so Rebekah could earn wages for her assistance. Recalls Kerry, "When I asked Rebekah what sort of privilege she planned on earning for this work, I expected to hear her say something like a Happy Meal at McDonald's. But I knew we were teaching her the right real estate lessons when, instead, she piped up cheerfully: 'A horse property!'"

108. WHITE KNIGHT OF EXPERIENCE

Experienced investors can come to the rescue through
step-by-step problem solving.

■ ■ ■

Dan Auito (http://www.magicbullets.com) has a friend—"an
intelligent perfectionist"—who had built a house himself, a solid structure through and through. It was built so well, when the energy rating
text, called a blow test, was conducted, the house had no air leaks.

Dan knew who had built the house, the quality of construction,
its energy rating, and its value based on what his friend had sold it
for to new owners, a couple from New Jersey. Originally, they paid
$159,000. The neighbor told Dan about the family, their habits, the
upgrades, and modifications they made to the home. In his opinion,
this couple acted "a little squirrelly" with their habits and design
choices. For example, they had installed a spiral staircase and painted
it a fuchsia purplish-pink—which alone would turn off more than
one potential buyer. The original paint had pencil and marker lines
scribbled here and there, the faucets and caulking needed repair, the
glass in a kitchen cabinet was missing, the walls needed new paint,
and the yard was overgrown. Although these problems were all cosmetic, most prospective buyers couldn't look past it.

After living in the house five years, the sellers were transferred
and got a relocation company involved in the transfer. Then they
contracted a local real estate agent who works at real estate half days
and delivers newspapers the other half (not too professional). This
agent seemed to bobble almost everything from the day the sellers
left. He did nothing to prepare the home to show well—he even left
an inflatable swimming pool/fun center half-deflated with stagnant
water and breeding mosquitoes at the entryway stairs. What a first
impression. What an easy fix, too.

By some stroke of luck, the agent found someone willing to pay $156,000 for this eyesore, but unfortunately, he couldn't come up with proper documentation for the original well and septic approval. Therefore, the relocation company sent its own engineer to backtrack. Doing this blew the deal clear out of the water, because the engineer didn't know local protocol and couldn't find the original paperwork, either. As a result, the potential buyers backed out, and the house sat empty for six months. Meanwhile, the relocated owners in New Jersey had to keep paying the mortgage while facing percolation tests for a special $10,000 septic tank.

This scene describes a classic stigmatized home, its value plummeting, its costs rising, and the agent worn out with phone calls, septic tank manufacturers, engineers, state regulators, cancelled contracts, and constant groaning from the sellers.

Enter Dan, the white knight—the educated investor—someone who knows what to do!

Dan continues the story: "What finally drove me to act was a call that presented an endgame for the situation. That is, a military officer asked if I had a place he could rent for two years. It got the wheels moving. I told him I'd get back to him."

Dan inspected the property and got an idea of what repairs needed to be made, mostly cosmetic. Then he questioned the agent and received every scrap of insider information that could legally be disclosed. "After my research, I knew that this property could be had for $137,000. Additionally, I would get a 3.5 percent commission, and the seller would pay the closing costs. I lined up this solid, two-year tenant willing to pay $1,350 a month plus utilities. An appraisal had been done six months earlier on the deal that had fallen through, and it had pegged the value at $160,000."

Dan still had to get the original documentation from the owner-builder to resolve the septic issue. "I called my friend who built the house, and he said, 'I have all the paperwork right here. The agent never asked me for it.' I looked it over and saw that he had the original design and construction survey, the engineer's original approval of the well and septic, the building department's approval, and the department of environmental conservation's waiver granting permission to install according to the plans. This completely removed all obstacles to financing, and the appraiser agreed."

Amazingly, problems that the agent had stewed over were solved in less than two hours!

Next, Dan had the lieutenant sign a two-year lease, including a check for one-and-a-half month's rent up front plus the last month-and-a-half of rent as a security deposit for a total of $4,050.00. Then Dan bought the house, painted, cleaned, trimmed, and tweaked it in only eight days.

"It is now a beautiful showplace on 1.77 acres and worth $27,000 more than I paid for it. In addition, there is a positive cash flow of $300 a month above my mortgage and escrow payment obligation."

The spiral staircase, repainted white, stands as a beautiful centerpiece in a home that anyone could be proud of! All it needed was a vision, some labor, and lots of paint.

Dan summarized what he learned from this transaction with these points of advice.

- Research and obtain as much history on the property as you can.
- Pay attention to the quality of construction and types of materials used.
- Use comparable sales, costs of construction, recent sales prices, assessments, and existing appraisals. Take into account the cost to cure existing defects in determining a reasonable value.
- Look for easily correctable problems that turn people off, then correct them.
- Pay attention to landscaping and how to improve its appearance.
- Analyze the events that led up to the sale and the seller's current position.
- Have a plan or endgame in mind for using the property once you acquire it.

- Always offer less than the full asking price. Be prepared to walk away if you don't get the price and terms that justify the purchase.
- Stay abreast of market conditions and events. Be patient; these deals will come your way when you're prepared to see them.

109. SPEAK KINDLY OF COMPETITORS

When you avoid bad-mouthing competitors, you can
sometimes help yourself.

■ ■ ■

Don and Joni Schaeffer had recently purchased a 15-year-old, 1,400-square-foot, three-bedroom, one-and-a-half-bath brick house. The previous owner actually called the Schaeffers and several other investors to see if they wanted to buy her house as an investment. The Schaeffers quickly returned her call, and when they found out that other investors were interested, they hurried over. The house was meticulously clean—so clean that you could have eaten off the floor. She said she just needed to move—she wanted out.

The house was in Fairview Heights, an up-and-coming neighborhood, so the Schaeffers thought it would be a good buy. But the seller had promised to show it to two other investors as well. When she told the Schaeffers that, Don asked for the names of the other two investors. He knew one of them—a man who was a good friend and a fellow member of their local investment group. Don told the lady to expect some fair offers from these people. He then asked her to call his wife and him after the other investors had made their offers.

Three hours after the Schaeffers had left her home, the lady called them. Because Don had spoken so kindly of his competitors, she'd decided to accept the Schaeffer's offer of $92,000 over the others' offers. The other investors had expressed concern about termites. The Schaeffer's subsequent inspection revealed an active infestation in one board in the crawlspace. That was certainly no big deal. They fixed that problem, installed new siding on the house for $2,000, shampooed the carpet, and subsequently resold the house for $125,000.

A kind word about competitors actually made all the difference to the Schaeffers in this situation.

110. SOLVING PROBLEMS WITHOUT BREAKING RULES

At times, you just have to think outside the box—
or outside your yard.

■ ■ ■

Many years ago, investor John Hanson (a pseudonym) bought a house on a large parcel of land. The back edge of the land sloped steeply down to an alley below the house. The neighborhood was not exactly the best, and the parcel of land had, in fact, been owned by a person with a penchant for grand theft auto. Years before, the owner had stripped radios, hubcaps, and other portable items from dozens of cars. He then allowed the stripped cars to coast down the sloped backyard and pile up just short of the alley.

When John bought the house and land, he, of course, saw all of the cars. He checked out their ownership and discovered that they were stolen and stripped, so he called the police department. The police investigated and, apparently because the cars were old and because they had more important things to do, they decided to do nothing about them. The police didn't want to deal with them, and the city wouldn't tow them because they were on private property.

But John wanted to get rid of the cars, so he thought long and hard about what to do. He came up with a plan. Over several months, he periodically drove down the alley and, using a logging chain to attach one of the stolen cars to his four-wheel drive vehicle, he dragged them into the alley one by one. After he'd leave a car there, he would call the authorities and anonymously report that someone had left a car parked in the middle of the alley. The city would immediately dispatch a tow truck.

John doesn't think anyone had a problem with this solution that seemed so obvious—especially the tow truck drivers. After all, the cars that just happened to be "parked" in the alley near his property had previously been parked on his property for all to see. And it was clear that at least one of the rusty cars couldn't have really been driven, because it had no tires. Still, John managed to drag it into the alley.

John had focused on how the people working for the city could relate to his problem and not go against city ordinances. As a result, he found a way to make them see his problem as their own.

111. INVESTOR AS RESCUER

Look for nonmonetary ways to help sellers.

■ ■ ■

Ginny Pitts had purchased a five-bedroom, two-bath, brick ranch house on a large lot from a retiring couple moving to the countryside. As Ginny walked through the house for the first time, she was accosted by the strong stench of cigarette smoke coming from the lower level. She found her way to the basement and saw a young man and woman—the son and daughter of the owners—chain-smoking while they played video games. They barely lifted their heads from the television screen when their mother introduced them to Ginny.

Back upstairs, the retiring couple proudly showed Ginny a Fleetwood Homes brochure and pointed out the teal-and-rose-toned, singlewide trailer they had already ordered. Ginny noticed the home's floor plan had no room for the son and daughter, so she asked, "Just the two of you will be moving? When are your children moving out?" The couple looked nervously at each other. Then, with shifting eyes and shuffling feet, they told her that they weren't sure. Suddenly Ginny understood. The couple was moving because their children had returned to the nest to mooch off of them. The older couple was highly motivated by the thought of having peace and quiet in a new, smoke-free space!

The couple quickly accepted the investor's offer of $75,000 and request for a quick closing. On the day that they closed, Ginny notified their children that they had to move and started eviction proceedings. Luckily for everyone, they moved on without much delay.

112. CONFESSIONS OF A QUADRIPLEGIC INVESTOR

No matter who you are, where you live, how much money you have, how old you are, or even how disabled or abled you are, you, too, can succeed at real estate.

■ ■ ■

Dustin Godnick, who is paralyzed from the chest down, has this incredibly poignant story to share.

"At age 17, I was heavily into drugs and alcohol, but a miracle happened one night when I was drinking. This miracle gave me a second chance at life.

"My friends and I were driving to a club to go dancing, and a BMW pulled up beside my friend's BMW. Both cars took off as if they were competing in a drag race. We were going around a turn, and both cars slid out of control, putting our car into a tree. I was in the back seat. At the moment of impact, the passenger seat unlatched and hit me in the jaw, breaking it and my neck. I got flown to the hospital and spent a lot of time learning how to use my newly paralyzed body.

"A few years later, I was given a book that changed my life: *Rich Dad, Poor Dad,* by Robert T. Kiyosaki with Sharon L. Lechter. After reading it, I was hooked on finding financial independence and gaining a life of plenty. I started asking the right questions of the right people and found a mentor willing to help. My mentor was a paraplegic (paralyzed from the waist down) and had also lost his eyesight. Together, we completed more than 12 deals in less than a year, plus I have accumulated 3 rental units of my own and have done very well.

"Through my experience, I believe that anyone who has the right desire and motivation can accomplish anything. I mean anything. Remember, I am paralyzed from the chest down and only 20 years old. My business partner is blind and in a wheelchair, yet he handles several other real estate ventures on the side. If we can do it, so can you."

■ TIPS

97. Any investment that you can add value to, realize tax benefits from, and actually see and touch should be a good one.

98. It's never too late to start becoming a real estate investor.

99. Finding creative ways to lease properties puts more money in your pocket.

100. You never really know what impression you are making on a prospective seller.

101. You'll never know it all, but you can learn enough.

102. Build a power team of professionals who understand your investment goals and style.

103. When appropriate, take the opportunity to perform a great service for owners, for neighborhoods, and for families that need a new direction.

104. Making good money in real estate can cause you to confront deeply hidden beliefs from your past regarding your self-worth and the concept of being rich. These deserve your attention and honest self-evaluation.

105. Understand that if you never ask, you'll never receive.

106. Make your portfolio more profitable by partnering with a knowledgeable and reliable property manager.

107. Teach your children how to invest early in life.

108. Experienced investors can come to the rescue through step-by-step problem solving.

109. When you avoid bad mouthing competitors, you can sometimes help yourself.

110. At times, you just have to think outside the box . . . or outside your yard.

111. Look for nonmonetary ways to help sellers.

112. No matter who you are, where you live, how much money you have, how old you are, or even how disabled or abled you are, you too can succeed at real estate.

SUGGESTED READING

Auito, Dan. *Magic Bullets in Real Estate.* Self-Published. Available online at http://www.magicbullets.com.

Conti, Peter and David Finkel. *Making Big Money Investing in Real Estate without Tenants, Banks, or Rehab Projects.* Chicago: Dearborn Trade Publishing, 2002.

Goodwin, Daniel, Richard Rusdorf, and Barbara McNichol. *The Landlord's Handbook: A Complete Guide to Managing Small Investment Properties.* Chicago: Dearborn Trade, 2004.

Norman, Jan. *What No One Ever Tells You about Marketing Your Own Business: Real Life from 101 Successful Entrepreneurs.* Chicago: Dearborn Trade Publishing, 2004.

Norman, Jan. *What No One Ever Tells You about Starting Your Own Business: Real Life Start-Up Advice from 101 Successful Entrepreneurs.* Chicago: Dearborn Trade Publishing, 2004.

Shemin, Robert. *Secrets of a Millionaire Real Estate Investor.* Chicago: Dearborn Trade Publishing, 2000.

Thornton, Rosemary Fuller. *The Reality of Real Estate: What You Don't Know about Investing in Real Estate Can Bankrupt You.* Charlottesville, VA: Hampton Roads Publishing, 1993. Available online at http://www.gentlebeampublications.com.

Government

- *U.S. Department of Housing and Urban Development (HUD)* (http://www.hud.gov). HUD's mission is to increase home ownership, support community development, and increase access to affordable housing free from discrimination.
- *U.S. Department of Veterans Affairs (VA) Home Loan Guaranty Services* (http://www.homeloans.va.gov). VA Home Loan Guaranty Services may allow veterans to obtain loans with extraordinarily low interest rates and without down payments.
- *Freddie Mac* (http://www.freddiemac.com). Freddie Mac purchases single-family and multifamily residential mortgages and mortgage-related securities, which it finances primarily by issuing mortgage pass-through securities and debt instruments in the capital markets.
- *Fannie Mae* (http://www.fanniemae.com). Fannie Mae's public mission, and defining goal, is to help more families achieve the American dream of home ownership.
- *U.S. Department of Commerce Census Bureau* (http://www.census.gov). The Census Bureau serves as the leading source of quality data about the nation's people and economy.

Financing

- Bank Rate (http://www.bankrate.com). BankRate.com is a one-stop Internet resource for mortgage rates, CD rates, auto loans, credit cards, mortgages, personal finance advice, and more.

Associations

- *Georgia Real Estate Investors Association* (http://www.gareia .org). America's largest real estate investor group assists its members in succeeding in their real estate investment plans by providing continuing education, motivation, and opportunity in a positive and mutually supportive environment.
- *Real Estate Investors of Nashville (Tennessee)* (http://www .reintn.net). REIN is a nonprofit association open to anyone, whether beginner or professional, with an interest in real estate investing. It is devoted to helping members learn, grow, and prosper as real estate investors.
- *The National Association of Realtors* (http://www.realtor.com). The official site of the National Association of Realtors.
- *The National Real Estate Investors Association* (http://www .nationalreia.com). The National Real Estate Investors Association works with local investor groups to share resources and exchange information.

Franchising

- *HomeVestors* (http://www.homevestors.com). HomeVestors is the national real estate investment franchise that proclaims on so many bright yellow billboards "We Buy Ugly Houses."

Writing/Editing

- *Barbara McNichol Editorial* (http://www.barbaramcnichol .com). Highly recommended manuscript editorial services.

Specializes in real estate subjects and and offers Word Trippers reference e-book.

- *Sherry Sterling* (sterling@dakotacom.net). Manuscript editor and proofreader.

Marketing

- *Kinko's* (http://www.kinkos.com). Kinko's mission is to provide document solutions—done right, anytime, anywhere.
- *VistaPrint* (http://www.vistaprint.com). VistaPrint's mission is to provide premium affordable, convenient, and quality printing for everyone.

International Real Estate Investing

- *REALS.com* (http://www.reals.com). REALS.com is a one-stop Internet resource for a wide variety of international and domestic real estate activities.

Investor Community Sites

- *American Investors in Real Estate Online* (http://www.aireo .com). The #1 most visited real estate investor Web site.
- *Creative Real Estate Online* (http://www.creonline.com). Creative Real Estate Online has offered real estate investing information on the #1 real estate investment Web site since 1995.
- *DealmakersCafé.com* (http://www.dealmakerscafe.com). DealmakersCafé.com is a one-stop Internet resource for real estate investing for the real estate investor wanting to succeed.
- *FSBO.com* (http://www.fsbo.com). FSBO.com provides an Internet-based sales listing service for real estate owners.
- *MR. LANDLORD* (http://www.mrlandlord.com). MR. LAND-LORD offers free rental forms, management software, real estate books, and landlord advice to better manage and lease rental property.

People who contributed their stories or helped collect stories for this book:

- Amber Ferguson
- Barbara Downing
- Barbara McNichol (http://barbaramcnichol.com; editor@ barbaramcnichol.com)
- Calvin Keeton
- Charles Benn (creativerealestateproperties@msn.com)
- Court Gettel
- Craig Schiesser
- Dale Hire
- Dan Auito (http://www.magicbullets.com; MagicBullets @Alaska.com)
- Dave Altman (dave@altmanteam.com)
- David Finkel (http://www.resultsnow.com; David @ResultsNow.com)
- Donn and Joni Schaeffer (1buyhouses@msn.com)
- Doug Simpson (http://www.erahillwood.com; dsimpson@ realtracs.com)
- Doug Traxler
- Dustin Godnick (wheelz192003@yahoo.com)
- Gary and Clara Hill
- Ginny Pitts (http://www.grandcanyonproperties.com; Ginny @GrandCanyonProperties.com)
- Glen and Kathy Marks

- Hal Wilson (http://www.thewilsonrealestategroup.com; Wilson@mtrmls.com)
- Jeanne Hoechst-Ronner
- Jeff Gaw (jdgaw@comcast.net)
- Jeff Petracco (jpetracco@aol.com)
- Jim Greeley (http://www.greyhoundproperties.com; info@ greyhoundproperties.com)
- John Lay (jlconstruction@charter.net)
- John and Mercedes Rezvanpour (http://www.remax.com)
- John Weary
- Joyce Bone (http://www.juiceplusguru.com; Joycebone1 @yahoo.com)
- Judy Cook and Chris Christie (http://www.twincreekbb.com; Stay@TwinCreekbb.com)
- Kerry Baird
- Kim Sandell
- Kris Bender
- Larry E. Elliott
- Lee Kerger
- Matt Fletcher (http://www.miproperty.com; detroithomeinspector@yahoo.com)
- Maureen Bream
- Pat Kiehl (http://www.foreclosuredepot.com; info@ 4closuredepot.com)
- Phil Pelletier (pcpelletier@msn.com)
- Renée Margaret
- Rob Baker
- Robert Shemin (http://www.robertshemin.com)
- Rosemary Fuller Thornton (http://www. gentlebeampublications.com)
- Rusty and Velma Edwards
- Stephen Starbuck (678-714-6611)
- Steve Slone (SteveSloane@Comcast.net; 615-618-1608)
- Susan Benting
- Terri and Jason O'Saile

- Thomas Brynner
- Tom Hamilton
- Vicki Bianchi
- Vinny Ribas (http://www.ibinashville.com; Vinny@IBINashville.com)

Share the message!

Bulk discounts
Discounts start at only 10 copies and range from 30% to 55% off retail price based on quantity.

Custom publishing
Private label a cover with your organization's name and logo. Or, tailor information to your needs with a custom pamphlet that highlights specific chapters.

Ancillaries
Workshop outlines, videos, and other products are available on select titles.

Dynamic speakers
Engaging authors are available to share their expertise and insight at your event.

Call Dearborn Trade Special Sales at 1-800-621-9621, ext. 4444, or e-mail trade@dearborn.com.

Dearborn™
Trade Publishing
A **Kaplan Professional** Company